D1531472

RAISED BED GARDENING FOR STARTERS

THE ULTIMATE GUIDE TO SUCCESSFULLY BUILDING YOUR OWN HEALTHY AND PRODUCTIVE GARDEN IN JUST 3 DAYS

BELLE TAYLOR

A Special Gift To Our Readers

Included with your purchase of this book is Your Harvest Recipe.
You will be getting 15 very simple and easy delicious recipes as you work and do magic in your kitchen from your backyard's harvest!

Visit the link RIGHT NOW and claim your FREE bonus gift!

belletaylorbooks.com

For paperback versions only:
Scan the QR code for an access
to colored pictures!

CONTENTS

INTRODUCTION

Have you decided to create your own garden? The thought of your hands in the soil, the smell of the damp earth, the blossoms, the tomatoes, the tall shrub privacy - whatever your dream raised bed garden might be, you've come to the right place.

I couldn't be happier for you!

Sprouting seedlings and seeing them grow as the seasons unfold is something I've enjoyed for many years. Sharing ideas, experiences, successes, and yes, failures, makes it all the more fun. Although, a raised bed garden is a very wise choice. You will be eliminating many of the headaches known to traditional gardeners.

Raised box gardening is a smart way to build a bed. It's like bringing the tried and true methods of traditional gardening into modern-day logic. You will be able to experience the ease of maintenance, reap the benefits of updated irrigation methods, and plant the hardiest of varieties. Additionally, you will also be experiencing tried and true methods of planting and harvesting organically, which have been handed down for decades, if not millennia. You can also plant edibles - the ability to harvest enough food for a family to preserve will provide a bounty of off-season enjoyment.

Though raised bed gardening has been used for many years now, the development of drip irrigation, organic processes, and trending landscape designs has raised garden awareness to a more practical and effective level than ever before. Raised boxes are also a beautiful focal point in any garden or landscape.

There are so many uses for a raised bed garden, too!

Your *raised garden* can consist of

- a corner box on the edge of your backyard deck
- a newly timbered square, cordoned off to grow luscious tomatoes for your bountiful table and out-of-season enjoyment
- small shrubs in a raised bed can section off a

boundary in your yard, creating a green and beautiful "fence"

- a curved and raised bed that can protect a collection of prize roses, providing you with beautiful blooms while keeping playing children safe from tossing the ball over
- a huge raised bed with perfectly calculated soil to grow melons and vine trailing vegetables for an organic and pest-free harvest

The options and benefits of a raised bed are numerous, and you will not regret your decision to have one. Even if you don't like where your bed is, moving it can be extremely easy. Simply put the soil in a large can, move the frame to your new spot, and refill the bed with soil from the can.

Transplanting from a raised bed is also less traumatic on the plants. By having well-thought-out designs to ease the digging and transfer of sensitive root balls, rhizomes, or corms, your raised bed could be a "staging" area for later planting strong plants in other parts of your yard.

All in all, once you begin constructing a raised bed, you will be thinking of your *next* project before you complete your first.

And after you've experienced the first?

Well, don't be surprised if you find yourself with several raised beds by the end of the season.

The benefits are many, and the constraints are few.

Gardening in a raised bed is quite like gardening in an elitist environment. By having your plants in a raised bed, you eliminate many of the gardening woes normally found in ground-level gardens.

- Pests are less intrusive, including bugs, meandering rodents, and, I dare say, the digging puppy.
- Soil conditions are controlled, giving you the freedom to have a garden even if your soil isn't particularly good, without the monumental task of amending your entire yard's soil, year after year.
- Watering systems are more efficient and easier to repair while keeping plants consistently hydrated.
- Staking, trellising, and general corralling of your incredibly prolific plants is easier and less time consuming.
- Yards and gardens can be organized into areas and "rooms" with thriving, beautiful beds, multi-level varieties, and season after season of variety and options.

- Keeping plants protected from extreme weather, both pre-growth and post-growth season, is easier and more successful.
- Maintaining your garden is easier on your body physically, with easier digging and less bending over.

- **And No Weeds!**

I'm sure you've noticed, there are many types of raised garden beds, and they can be in place for many different reasons.

There are low-rise beds from 4–6 inches tall. These provide a small barrier for plants while giving them the benefit of deep soil rooting. There are slightly higher beds, 6–16 inches, which not only protect plants but separate areas of the garden into specific sections, guiding the eye to larger landscapes. There are terraced beds that create fences, barriers, and permanent borders. And taller still, there are elevated beds with an airflow beneath them, giving plants a totally controlled environment while also helping ease back trauma or weed determination.

Whatever your reasons for wanting a raised bed garden, you've come to the right place! In this book, I will teach you how to construct a raised bed in the most economical way with no hazardous treated wood to ensure an organic environment. I will assist you in creating a decorative bed that will meld with your landscape and established design.

I will also show you the best way to irrigate your bed for optimal distribution and conservation of water, get the most from a Do-It-Yourself design, construct a drip irrigation bed to get the most water to your plants with minimal effort, and detail the necessities and benefits of an automatic timed system.

You will understand the reasoning behind the do's and don'ts of gardening and learn to expand your own skills without having to look up every plant, every zone, and every light preference. Your bed will be stationary. Your plants will thrive in a predetermined environment. So many considerations, usually dealt with in a yard or landscape, are eliminated when growing with raised bed gardening.

You will also learn about soil composition - what types of soil mix and compost to use for different kinds of plants and production, and how to keep your raised bed producing wonderful and healthy plants, season after season.

Lastly, you will learn how to "rest" your bed for seasonal hibernation, giving your raised box a well-deserved break while rejuvenating the soil for the next season's spectacular show.

With a little bit of pre-planning, raised bed gardening will be your favorite and most successful way to grow vegetable gardens, begin seedlings, nurture small perennials, create a living fence, and much more.

Let's begin creating your perfect raised bed garden!

1

WHAT KIND OF RAISED BED DO YOU WANT?

D igging into the soil creates a calmness unlike any other therapy I know.

The smell of the peat.

The coolness of the dirt.

The life potential of what I hold in my hand.

And the promise of "what may be."

All of these sensations call to hundreds, if not thousands or millions, of gardeners to don gloves, grab a shovel, and turn yards of dirt every spring, summer, fall, and if lucky, winter into natural havens. A promise of green, lush plants, tasty vegetables, and colorful blooms dance in our minds just as sugarplums dance in children's dreams at Christmas time.

But the raised bed gardener experiences are a doubled amount of glee because there is little work, little weeding, and little upkeep. It is the ultimate luxury of gardening.

Whether you are looking to plant a window box under your kitchen window or row upon row of boxed crops, raised bed gardening promises ten-fold the return of typical landscape gardening with half of the effort.

And why is this, you ask?

Number one, you are the master of the dirt!

Because the soil is *the* major ingredient of a successful garden, it is imperative any gardener gives their plants a rich, specialized soil in which to grow. That is if they want to make the most of their dedicated time, specific planning and consistent nurturing with supplies and water is necessary. The gardener's job is not an easy task, but when using the resources a raised bed can provide, they are many steps closer to the "perfect condition" for which gardeners are constantly searching.

Raised Box Material

When first considering a raised bed, you need to decide on the materials you will be using to construct your box(es). Before you set your mind on what you will be constructing *with*, let's discuss the many choices you have and the benefits or detriments each can provide.

Wood

Most often, raised beds are made from wood. If you are leaning to this material, make sure you are using untreated, bare wood. If there are finishes or paint on it or it is "treated" timber (to keep insects or rot from destroying the outside use), stay clear of these for your raised beds, especially if you intend to plant edibles. These finishes will leach into the soil. Even if they don't kill your plants, the plant will absorb them and, therefore, store them in the foliage, blooms, and fruit. From there, they can find their way into your lungs, skin, and digestive system.

Use new, untreated wood. Yes, it probably will rot sooner than treated wood, but knowing that you are growing the healthiest plants you can, especially if you are going to all the work to plant, water, and maintain them, would be your most advantageous choice. Wood also takes time to rot, even in the moistest of conditions. So, at the very least, you can count on an average of five years or more of well-constructed and fully functional boxes. In fact, I've had a wood box for over 20 years. The patina and its characteristics make the box all the more charming as the years pass, in addition to giving me the peace of mind of knowing the plants are free of toxins and chemicals.

These boxes are quite easy to move if you find you want to redesign or move the raised bed to another part of your garden. The wood's weight is no heavier than a table, and the construction is sturdy enough to be done by two people. Removing the soil to a tarp or wheelbarrow will make the job of refilling the dirt back in easier, so take care in placing it in a large enough area. Just empty the raised bed of soil, reposition the box, and refill!

By using wood, you are also giving the soil a way to "breathe," thereby making the dirt less vulnerable to packing or becoming too dense. If the soil can't breathe, it is harder for the roots to absorb water, spread, and thrive.

Instructions for Assembling a Simple 4' X 4' X 8" Wood Raised Garden Box Begin with untreated wood and 2 1/2" wood screws. If you have a power drill, you will be set, but you can put this together with a Phillips screwdriver also (driving the screws will need just a bit more strength). You will need -

- 2 - 1" X 8" X 8' untreated lumber (the least expensive, usually pine, will be fine).
- 4 - 2" X 4" X 8" untreated lumber pieces (quite often, you will be able to get "scrap" pieces of lumber at the home center or lumber yard. Sometimes, they will just include it, but you may also need to have a larger piece, a 4' length, cut into four sections.)
- 16 to 24 - 2 ½" wood screws, depending on the necessary strength of your raised box.
- Drill with Phillips screw head and ¼" drill bit or Phillips screwdriver.

While at the home center or lumber yard purchasing your lumber, have them cut the 8' timbers in half, giving you four pieces of lumber measuring 1" X 8" X 4'. If you need to have the 2" X 4" cut to 8" lengths, do this also.

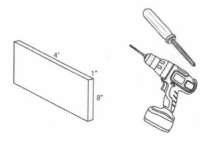

Mark out the location you want your garden box to be. Set planks of 1" X 8" wood on edge along your lines of the outside garden box, with the ends making an even corner, as pictured below.

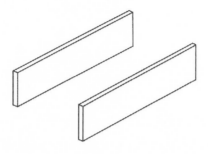

Set each corner level to the one butting up against it, drill two screw holes and screw in each screw. By doing this, you will take pressure off the wood when setting

the screws, thereby avoiding the possibility of splitting the wood. However, if you are using a hand screwdriver, this will work too. It might make the work a bit harder, but the slow setting of the screws will give the wood time to ease without splitting.

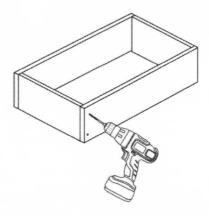

After you have finished all four corners, take a piece of 2" X 4" and set it inside each corner of your box.

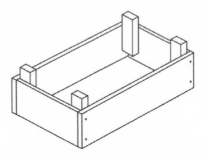

From the opposite side of the 1" X 8" corners, drill and set another two screws, this time drilling into the 2" X 4" instead of the other 1" X 8".

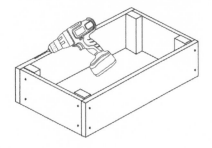

Your garden box will be strong enough to accommodate the square footage of soil and plants you will be planting if you do this. But if you'd like to substantiate the connections, another screw or two placed between the originals can add to the sturdiness of your raised bed.

With this simple construction, you can also adapt to different sizes and heights, as well as adding a corner piece over the 2" X 4" to keep the boards from shifting, or set longer 2" X 4" boards into the ground if you see fit.

A word about railroad ties - Though these items appear to be a great material to construct your raised beds from, don't use them. The chemicals they've been treated with (creosote) are particularly toxic to plants even if they are old or if you line your beds or re-treat them with a sealer. Inevitably, they will poison your plants, and make your raised bed a total failure. It would be better to use them as a path paver in places where you don't want any type of foliage to grow - *for about a 3-foot surround.*

Metal

If you are thinking of using metal sheeting or corrugated steel, make sure, once again, that there are no toxins or finishes on the metal, such as a rust inhibitor or solvent that keeps sheets from adhering to each other (usually an oil or varnish that lessens with time). Often, these boxes are cornered with wood, which is very attractive and gives an industrial look to your garden.

You could also use metal brackets with wood, which makes constructing the box quite easy too. Look for the brackets at your local home improvement center. If you are constructing your box yourself, make sure the bracket is on the *outside* of the box. This will not only make it easier to construct but will provide air, so the metal doesn't rust in the soil, keeping any galvanized or steel rust from affecting your plants while also giving the bracket a longer life.

Metal can inhibit the spread of roots due to the lack of air circulation in the soil, but this should be minimal, especially if the bed is larger than 4 square feet. Keep in mind that the more the soil is, the less the metals' density will affect plant roots. If you are looking, perhaps, to enlarge your box, this may be the reason to expand your garden box!

Metal boxes tend to be on the heavier side, so if you think you might need to move yours in the future, factor the weight into your final decision.

Rock

The first material used for raised beds, rock will give you a natural look while also containing the soil, although this depends on how close your stones sit to each other and if you have an inside liner keeping the soil from

seeping out when you water. Many rock beds are used as landscape boundaries and provide definition in a yard or separate walking paths from picturesque beds.

A well-constructed rock-raised bed or wall (think curved bed in front of a fence or home) is one of the most visually appealing materials you can use. And if you are using perennials or planting a hedge or barrier within the box, the natural look of rock can give definition and "tidiness" to a yard, no matter the height. Plants that spread and creep over the tops of these beds are always attractive and can help keep soil in place on slopes and terraced gardens.

Rock beds are considered to be more permanent than wood, metal, or synthetic material boxes, so if you are going to move them in the near future, you may want to rethink rock. Most of the time, they take longer to construct and can be taxing on a gardener's back. When you place rocks in your garden for any use, be sure you are putting them where they can spend a good amount of their lives!

Man-made Materials

There are so many bed edgings, panels, and kits to assemble raised beds. I could begin here and complete the entire book by just discussing them all. When using these materials, you will have to decide what your end purpose will be before you make your financial choice.

Details to consider are:

- Ease of installation (usually the most attractive advantage)
- Aeration and health of the soil
- Possible oils or toxins on the material for packing and shipping benefits
- Durability and upkeep for visual aesthetics and performance
- Costs

- Return policy

You probably think I'm not a proponent of plastic or resin box designs - and that would be incorrect. I do think they have a place in the garden, especially in raised bed plantings. I do, however, believe that sometimes they can disappoint, so make sure you consider all the details I mentioned above before putting one of these types of boxes in your garden. Plastic or resin tends to be more expensive than other materials of box construction and often disappoint the purchaser in more than one area. There are great containers available, but there are a lot of shabby ones too. You don't want poorly constructed ones assembled with less than adequate material that will lose their good looks in outdoor weather. Ensure there is a good guarantee and refund policy if your purchase doesn't stand the test of time.

You may also find elevated garden boxes in plastics and decking material, which can be easy to put together and provide a cohesive look to a patio. Most of the time, these boxes are on the small side, and some may even be considered as window-box size. If using these types, make sure there is lots of peat in your soil and grow plants that will do well in these types of boxes, such as annuals, vines, and some bulbs. The soil won't be able to breathe very well, so having an aerated compost would be wise.

Brick and Cut Stone

Like rock, using heavier materials such as brick and stone, create a more permanent bed for your gardening. Using bricks and cut stone creates a more defined and formal look. They are often used in courtyards, desert and gravel landscapes, and footpaths.

I've used bricks in many of my landscape-raised beds because I had a bunch of them left over when I replaced brick paths with natural stone pavers. But more importantly because I found that I can dry-stack them for temporary use before committing to formal rock or stonewalls, in case I didn't like it. If it was temporary, I could disassemble the box and move it somewhere else.

Bricks and carved stone can give you a good idea of a design without having to haul large rocks around, while still giving you the possibility of moving them when they don't work out.

Bricks come in many different types, and some are much more porous than others. Some may have a "finish" on them, while others shouldn't be used in colder climates (freeze-thaw conditions). Be aware of the kind of bricks or stones you are considering and make sure they will conform to the type of use you are planning, as well as annual outdoor weather conditions.

Concrete, Blocks, and Pavers

The most permanent and indestructible raised bed design would have to be made from poured concrete. If you are absolutely sure of where you want your beds or are thinking of incorporating walls, water features, or fountains, you may want to consider concrete. I'm not going to go into all the water feature needs here, but if you want to use concrete, you are probably already aware of the differences between the mixes, such as concrete vs. cement vs. waterproofing vs. many other options available.

Whatever feature you are designing, talk to professionals about the functionality of your design, your expectations, the types of plants you will be planting, and the longevity you are hoping for. You will also want to discuss the ease of mixing, prep, and construction.

Cement blocks are also a more permanent means to build a bed, and I've often seen some creative ideas for using them, stacked every which way, to provide crevices for tumbling ground cover and "mini pots" for other types of plants. Again, consider the material and make sure it won't kill your plants.

I have also seen some creative boxes made from pavers, either tipped on their side and dug halfway into the ground or glued together with construction adhesive. If you are a craft designer and have something in mind, you are probably halfway there already. If not, pavers can give you an easy way of assembling a box, but you need to realize that there probably isn't much of a chance of salvaging a box if you will be moving it often. Pavers are made to lie flat on the ground, and making them do otherwise can be challenging and test your patience.

Chapter Summary

- Constructing a raised bed garden box can be simple and easy, and accomplished in under an hour.
- Choose your box construction material wisely, and it will serve you well for many years.

In the next chapter, you will learn how to get water to your plants easily and effectively.

2

IRRIGATION AND WATERING AS EASY AS A TURN OF THE SPIGOT

Your raised beds will need their own source of water unless you design the location to receive water from a pre-sourced or established sprinkler system. Consider this - when your plants are large and full, it will be challenging for them to receive water at the roots, where it is most needed. Sprinklers can work, but be aware of the needs of your larger, more mature plants.

You may also think you won't have to set up a watering system if your raised bed is only a board or two up from ground level, but this can be hazardous to your plants' health and well-being. Since you will have a soil full of nutrients that support your plants and their root systems, they will naturally reach across as well as down into the soil when growing and establishing themselves in the dirt. Most plants' major root systems don't grow strictly downward, aside from root vegetables. It's smart to plan for when your plants are at their peak of growth and their necessities.

From the Faucet to the Roots

You may be a firm believer in drip irrigation systems, or you may want to water your beds by hand. Whichever method you prefer (and we all have our favorites!), make sure you have considered the following details.

Timetable

It's true, having raised beds will decrease the nighttime parade of damaging insects and herbivores. However, just because they are raised off the ground doesn't mean all your plants are safe from snails, aphids, and powdery mildew, which are all lovers of water and moisture left on and around plants.

By timing your watering just before dawn, you can avoid standing water in puddles and unnecessary drops on your plant leaves. If you are in a hot climate, this early day moisture will also protect sensitive roots from drying out and large-leaved plants from becoming parched.

Let's go over the different types of irrigation methods you can use for your raised bed gardens.

Plan Your Design and System

The earlier you decide on the materials you are going to construct your raised beds with, the earlier you can finalize how you want to get water to the inside of your box. If you have wooden boxes, drilling a hole in the side is an easy way to run a PVC or rubber hose through, but if you are using any kind of semi-permanent or permanent material such as rocks, stone, concrete, or plastics for the construction of your box, pre-planning can save you time, effort, and a redesigning of your box construct.

If you are using established systems, such as sprinklers that already water your raised bed area, make sure the *entire box* will be watered, and the plants you put into the box are able to adapt to the timing schedule you have for your established system. If you only water your yard three times a week, you will need to make sure you have a way to water seedlings and new plants until they are established, as these small plants need more water to develop their stems, leaves, and roots. Additionally, be aware of your plants' heights as they grow. They may reach the back of the box in spring, but after the tomatoes grow taller, you may find that shorter beets and cucumbers behind them are blocked.

Plan an easy and functional way to direct water. Install PVC piping or a hose to the inside of the box, with a hose-end, pop-on nozzle, or its own water spigot. PVC pipes and hoses can be secured inside the box with hose clamps or electrical brackets. Don't count on the dirt to hold the piping or hoses in place. You will be digging, and plants will be growing, causing changes in the dirt pressure and weight. This will most likely move and rearrange any initial layouts.

Another important point to consider is using rainwater from a cistern or barrel or on-demand water. The travel from source to your boxes should be permanent to make your caring for the box garden easy and enjoyable.

You can find many different and specialized sprinkler parts at your home supply store or sprinkler manufacturer. See which parts appeal to you and assemble your system with the help of one of their professionals. Don't forget to seal the connections as you build your water lines and distribution.

Sprinklers

Having a top-supplied water source for your raised beds works well, especially if your plants will be tall when planted, like shrubs, large tomato plants, or trees. These types of plants need more water than a drip irrigation system can produce unless you want to water them for hours at a time. Be sure to check the needs of the plants you are adding to your beds and determine how much water you will need to keep them healthy and thriving.

If you can talk to a water professional, ask them about the different sprinkler options and how much water output each sprinkler head will give during a specified period, such as one gallon per hour.

Drip

Drip irrigation systems are becoming more and more popular, and for good reason. Not only do they conserve water, but they are also becoming easier to install, and people have greater success in maintaining their productivity than they did years ago. A decade or two ago, lines would often become plugged, spigots and emitters would break or fall apart, and weather conditions would play havoc on their longevity. But no more!

If you believe this type of system would be easy for you to install, research the options because your plants would love nothing more than to have water at the ready to their roots. While many plants thrive when watered by an above-ground system, they can develop problems and suffer from diseases common with sprinkler-system irrigation, such as powdery mildew, black spot, and aphids. Ground irrigation bypasses these problems, putting water directly into the soil. You may find the initial expense a tad high, but a properly planned and installed drip system will serve you and your plants' needs for many seasons.

Soakers

Personally, I use soakers all over my yard. It's not because I believe them to be the best way to water, but because I can get the needed water to the plants or shrubs quickly and design a permanent system when I get the rest of the yard planted. I buy plants in masses and try to get them in the ground as quickly as possible.

Soakers can be temporary or permanent. Like drip systems, they offer plants water placement directly where the plants need it - at the base of the plant so it can get to their roots easily. Although soakers have a wonderful place in my own system, they do present some problems.

- They need to be replaced regularly because soakers lie directly on the ground making them more susceptible to erosion and wear.
- They move easily. So, each time you water, it is a good idea to check to make sure the hose is still where you want it, especially if you have animals or children who can accidentally move them from their original place.
- They are more obvious than most watering systems. The black color of many soakers is fine, but some are colored, such as a sand color

or green, which can stand out more than your plants do.

Because soakers are easily moveable, they can be a godsend to those of us with little time and many options. I never quite know what I'm designing in the yard from season to season, so I like the temporary option. If you like them and want a permanent answer, there are wire stakes or U-shaped hooks that can stake down the hose to keep it from moving, giving you a more reliable irrigation method.

Hoses

I am always amazed when I see people using hoses to water their gardens, but after a water main broke on my automatic system, I realized why many people still use hoses with sprinklers or a hand-held nozzle. Spending time in the garden while placing a hose and sprinkler gives you time to look around without the notion of doing anything else than watering, which I find relaxing. It also gives you time to listen to the birds, as they gather when the promise of water rises, as well as a close-up view of plants you would otherwise not get time for.

Maybe a tomato plant needs re-staking, or there is an infestation of whiteflies you can tend to before it gets out of control. This may have gone unnoticed until it develops into a larger problem.

What I'm trying to say is this - spending time on the end of a hose with a nozzle with nothing to do but water your beloved plants gives you a chance to view and experience your bed from a more relaxed and contemplative view. And it's a well-known fact that all plants benefit from a little extra tender, loving care.

PVC (plastic piping)

Putting together your own "sprinkler system" within a raised bed is easy and makes your life very simple, especially if you do it before planting. It is a permanent system, but if you are sure you will always want rows or the connection at the corner, you will probably want to investigate this type of system for your raised beds. It is efficient, inexpensive, and reliable. Installation is easy, and putting a timer on this system makes manually irrigating your beds a distant thought.

Many home centers and irrigation or sprinkler companies have professionals experienced in the use of these systems and can help you design yours with minimal effort and wonderful results. Make sure you have your measurements and heights of plant maturity when you decide on the design.

Drainage

When setting up your raised boxes, make sure you have proper drainage for your plants. If you are putting your box directly on the dirt, aerate the soil a bit by making holes into the ground, about 3" deep and about 6" apart, before setting the box on top. By doing this, you will keep water from puddling between your box's good soil and the poor soil at ground level. If water begins to congregate, it can cause mildew, increase deterioration of your structure, or create "wet feet" for your plants. This keeps them from thriving and eventually water-logs the root system, giving more than one kind of insect a wonderful place to call home.

Time Schedule

Timing the watering of your raised beds will depend heavily on the plants you have planted, and their age. If you are starting seedlings, you will want to keep the soil moist to increase their ability to develop roots and become strong, usually watering with a fine spray. If you have planted a row of arborvitae as a hedge, you will also want to keep them well-watered but on a consistent schedule, adhering to the planting instructions. They will need a more thorough, deep watering schedule so roots spread and they can grow without specific watering attention next season.

Timers

I love timers - they keep watch over my garden and beds when I can't, which I appreciate, living in a high desert plain. I can also, as I mentioned, set the timers to water my beds when the rest of the neighborhood is asleep, taking advantage of the higher water pressure and full coverage, as well as decreasing evaporation and insect preferences.

Many timers are available that can make your life easy, from one or two station timers you can connect to an outdoor house spigot, to phone app timers and ready to schedule 12-station landscape designs.

If you don't already have an idea about setting a timer on your system, consider one. Not only can they make your personal life easier, but they also deliver a consistent schedule and amount of water to your plants, which gives them every reason to grow to their peak form and provide you with the best results. They also keep water efficiency a priority, which your wallet will appreciate.

Providing the proper amount of water to plants in a raised bed is necessary, but it doesn't have to be a burden. If well planned in the initial designing phase, the small efforts will prove to be well worth your time, as you will see fantastic results as the season progresses.

Chapter Summary

- Using simple and easy watering systems will make your task of watering easier, guaranteeing consistent watering schedules and less wastage.
- Keep your system simple and effective.

In the next chapter, you will learn how to provide your plants with nutrition and support.

3

RICH SOIL FOR HAPPY, THRIVING PLANTS

W hile most gardeners believe soil is the "make or break" element in having a healthy and successful garden, most landscapers swear by soil supplements and doing everything to ensure that the soil is not only as nutritious as it can be but also that it "breathes."

Nutrients are to plants as vitamins are to people, and all plants benefit from the attention added conditioners provide. Whether you are a firm believer of organic nutrients, such as manure and emulsifications, or prefer easily distributed water-based plant food, whatever your vegetations' roots are sunk into will show in the vitality of their above-ground growth.

A Healthy Start

Any successful garden bed must begin with good soil. It is what gives a seedling the much-needed nurturing to grow into a healthy, strong plant.

You have many options for preparing and filling your raised beds. Because of the increased popularity in gardening of all types in recent years, soil conditioners and mixes have just as wide a range in variety and specialty uses.

Before you buy any soil mix or separate conditioners to create your own mix, research the plants you will be planting to make sure you include the needed nutrients and additives your plants will require.

A well-balanced soil mix will consist of granular dirt (crushed rock or topsoil), sand, loam, organic matter, and conditioners (perlite, water inhibitors, and specialty mixes).

If you are planting vegetables, make sure the mix has plenty of loam to keep the roots happy while also not constricting their space. If plants have to work to get their roots out, they will be small and weak. If you have root plants, such as carrots, potatoes, or peanuts, make sure the soil has a good draining consistency so the edible roots don't rot or get bugs because of retained water in the soil.

You will also want to pay close attention to acid-loving or alkaline-loving plants, like hydrangeas or ferns. Pay attention to the pH level of the soil to achieve ideal conditions for these specialty plants and bushes.

Whatever your needs, there is an element to add to the soil to make it perfect for growing the plants you have in mind. At this point, soil preparation is probably the most important yet least considered element of having a raised bed garden. Once you put the dirt in and plant your plants, there is no going back to make the soil better. Therefore, beginning with a great planting mixture is a prerequisite, in addition to being one of the reasons you are investing in a raised garden bed!

Do a bit of homework and find the ideal soil conditions for your raised beds. Doing so will mean your plants will return healthy crops and abundant blooms.

Let's talk about each element individually.

Water Drainage

As I've mentioned, drainage is important, not only for keeping our water costs in check but also for your plants' health. Keeping your plants well hydrated but not water-logged is important and is solely up to you when gardening in raised beds.

Make sure you have good draining soil. You can get this by adding ground rock (dirt or granular topsoil), sand (produces heavier soil while breaking up clay), or organic mulch (fir mulch, crushed eggshells, or ground husks). When pressing the soil together, you don't want it to keep its shape - it should fall loose in your palm. If it packs into a ball, add more sand or draining mulch until the consistency is right.

Loam and Soil

Rich, dark soil that doesn't pack down and is full of good nutrients and conditioners is called "loam," and every gardener strives for this. Fortunately, when gardening with raised beds, this feat is easily attainable simply because you are in total control of what your plants are growing in. You are filling it with "new" dirt.

Peat moss, soil pep, worm castings, steer manure, various guano, and potting soil will give you this, along with good topsoil from a well-maintained garden or plot. But be aware, not all bagged soils or bulk top-soil are the same. Most established retailers worth their weight will have the product's contents available for you to see and feel. If you are buying from a bulk supplier, you will be able to see it first-hand.

Depending on what you are viewing, the soil can be rich (steer manure or soil pep) or dry and full of "fillers" (some potting soil or mixes with fertilizer added). You may also see chalk (never good in any product unless it is straight gypsum) as one of the components.

An example of this is peat moss, which is fine if dry, as it will "plump" when watered. Some pre-mixes that have a considerable percentage of peat moss are dry too, to save on shipping costs. You may also see densely packed mixes. Most often, you will be able to tell almost immediately if the product is good or not, whether it is dry, compacted, moist, or has unknown ingredients in it. Read the labels, identify what might be contained, and if you have questions, ask the proprietor. They should be able to tell you what each ingredient is and the benefits it provides.

If you can't see the product directly, ask an associate to show you a sample. Sometimes they have samples in other areas of the garden center or store.

Don't ever buy any soil preparation without viewing the actual product. Buying soil products can be expensive. Additionally, you won't want anything in your raised bed that might be toxic, filler, or of poor quality. You will be spending time and money on this raised bed, and to take a risk on the soil is an unnecessary mistake.

If you are interested in purchasing products in bulk, many garden centers and landscape yards have huge bins with many kinds of compositions available. You will want to have a truck ready for them to load it in if you choose not to have it delivered (most often, they will have a delivery fee).

Pre-mix vs. Custom-Mix

If I'm going for a nutrient-filled soil with conditioners and slow-release feeding, I mix it with my own chosen products, combining one part peat moss, one part soil pep, and one part perlite or vermiculite (an aerator that keeps the soil from packing down). As I'm mixing it up, I add a bit of well-balanced plant food, 16-16-16 (the nitrogen, phosphorus, potash analysis), to assist not only blooming plants but vegetables too.

There are many pre-mixed products, and they may give you exactly what you believe your plants need. If you trust the mix and feel the sample you see is consistent with your needs, buying pre-mixed soil could be a great move for you. However, take into consideration the cost of such a pre-mixed product. They are often priced higher and offer little specifics for customizing for your plants, especially for blooming varieties or vegetables. You will probably need to buy just as many bags, if not more, to fill your bed(s) without the advantage of customizing the ingredients your specific plants will need.

If you buy separate soil types to mix specifically for your plants, you will be offering your plants the best soil to grow in and saving yourself some money. Because you will need many bags of products to fill your bed, buying them separately and mixing them in the bed will most likely give you exactly what you need while saving you money on expensive customized products that contain the same amount or lesser ingredients.

Organic

Organic gardening has taken the world by storm and has obviously given us reason to stop and compare techniques of feeding and caring for our plants. It proves to be not only the best proactive initiative for our plants but also for us as consumers of their bounty. It also eliminates the use of chemicals and toxins in our environment.

We are finding more and more residuals of previously used fertilizers, insecticides, and herbicides in our soils and groundwater than was ever imagined possible. The environment greatly suffers when we use toxins and chemicals. More often than not, an organic alternative works just as well, if not better than the chemically developed product. Nature was doing all this growing and maintaining the ecological balance long before we got here. We can always learn something new from using natural and organic methods of growing and maintaining productive gardens.

By using organic gardening techniques, organic plant food and soil conditioners, researchers have seen plants benefit. Additionally, insects and birds benefit too, with the natural balance of nature returning to a level of stability we have long forgotten is necessary.

Organic Feeding: Feed plants with fish emulsions, Epsom salts, worm castings, and composted material. Add these to your soil preparations and use them when your plants need bi-weekly feedings. Organic manures, guano, and droppings can also be of great benefit to your plants while also keeping insects (and animals) at bay. If you aren't aware of it yet, having earthworms in your soil is incredibly beneficial. By adding these super-heroes of soil conditioning, you will be organically adding profitable by-products to your soil while keeping it aerated and free of pests.

Natural Pest Control

Ridding your plants of unwanted insects while preserving the necessary ones can also give you a "natural protectant" while observing nature's requisite to stay balanced.

Release ladybugs and lacewings in your garden in the spring when the temperature is warm to keep many burrowing larvae, aphids, and grubs from harming young shoots, buds, and seedlings. This will also deter adult insects that can devastate a tomato harvest, fruit tree harvest, or rose blooms from becoming food for their taking.

Natural Weed Deterrents

Keep organic mulch on the top inch or two of your beds to not only reduce water evaporation but also deter snails and slugs from attacking your plants. A good organic mulch, such as composted fir mulch or other organic, soft compost, will ease your workload by suffocating weed seeds. Planting your plants closer together and in a circular fashion instead of rows or squares will also deter weeds from accessing light, which is another way of discouraging their germination and growth.

Time Release Nutrients

It used to be that these products only worked partially and were quite expensive. They have come a long way in developing time-release feeding, and taking advantage of that in your raised bed can be a wise move. You will notice that the products are a bit expensive, but they offer feeding on a continuous basis, which your plants will prefer, and eliminate the risk of skipping a feeding or two.

If you are a gardener who likes to dawdle in your garden (something I have been accused of being more than once!), time-released feeding may be excessive, as you will be hovering over the plants anyway. You might as well be feeding them a more robust organic fertilizer and give yourself an alibi for being in your garden.

Pre-mix or Custom-Mix

If I'm going for a nutrient-filled soil with conditioners and slow-release feeding, I would combine one part peat moss, one part soil pep, and one part perlite or vermiculite (an aerator that keeps the soil from packing down). As I'm mixing it up, I would add a bit of well-balanced plant food, 16-16-16 to govern not only blooming plants but also vegetables.

As I've said previously, don't spend a lot of money on a pre-mixed type of soil. Since you will need many bags to fill your bed, buying them separately and mixing them in the bed will give you specifically what you need while saving you money on expensive pre-mixed custom products that contain the same amount or lesser ingredients.

Coverage

Get a good idea of how much soil you will need for your raised bed by multiplying the length of your bed by its width, and then by its depth. This will give you how much soil you will need in a *cubic foot* measurement, which is the general measurement used when packaging garden products.

For example, if my raised box was 4' X 6' with a 2-feet depth, my calculations would look like this -

$$4' \text{ X } 6' \text{ X } 2' = 48 \text{ cubic feet}$$

When you get to your garden center, don't be shocked by the huge bags labeled as 4 cubic feet or 6 cubic feet. While they seem big, when you empty them into your box, you will be amazed at how little those large bags seem to fill. If you are unsure, get half the amount, but be prepared to go back a second time for necessary additions.

If you are using liter packaged products, note that 1 cubic foot = 28.32 liters.

Note: If you have elevated boxes or boxes that are deeper than your anticipated largest plants, consider filling the bottom of your boxes with inert filler, such as excess garden branches (with no bugs or fungus), large rocks, or other fillers that can take up space without having to fill the box with high-grade soil. You will save yourself money, and the plants will never reach the objects. Just make sure that the inert objects don't leach toxins into the soil or create hazards in the garden.

Chapter Summary

- Having good, rich soil for your plants is the key to a successful raised bed.
- Mixing your own combination of conditioners can save you money and time.

In the next chapter, you will learn how to safe-keep your garden from pests and infestations.

4

KEEPING THE CRITTERS OUT

Critters and creatures are the neighbors of your raised garden beds. And sometimes, they are the house guests who never seem to leave!

When we talk about insects or rodents, we often think of pests and intruders, but every so often, we are lucky enough to play hosts to beneficial creatures such as ladybugs, lace-wings, and our neighbors' predatory cat. By learning about your invasive visitors as well as the wonderful ones, you will be able to design, maintain, and enjoy your raised bed in the most optimal conditions possible. You will also be able to identify the "good bugs" from the bad ones while protecting your plants, the environment, and your harvest.

Harmful Insects

Most often, insects, including larvae and flying insects, can cause havoc to your plants and leave them looking wilted, discolored, and damaged. I'm going to discuss the main culprits here, but it would be a good idea to speak with your local extension service or a well-informed manager at a co-op, farmer's market, or farmers association for the pests that dominate your region and current season. Learn about the signs of infestation beforehand, so you will be able to act before a pest problem becomes unmanageable and steal your crops or blooms.

Aphids

These tiny insects are about the size of a pinhead and tend to gather in groups. You will often find them on young, succulent shoots and buds. They tend to take on the hue or color of the plants they are eating. They suck the sap from the plant, which gives them this appearance in addition to being a form of camouflage. Aphids cause your plants' foliage to become disfigured, and their excretion of sticky sap can cause sooty mold growth (cancerous lesions on stems and branches) on your plants. Often, a strong stream of water will wash off these bugs, but diligence while you do this is a must. Otherwise, you will just be spreading their infestation, as some will survive to eat again tomorrow.

Insecticidal soap, neem oil, and horticultural oil can help eliminate them, as can a homemade solution of dish soap, hot-pepper or garlic powder, and water (add 1 tablespoon dish soap, a dash of powder to 1 quart of water) sprayed on the insects. However, if your infestation has multiple generations, you will also have to treat your plants again, possibly two to three times, to be thorough.

Using native predators and parasites, such as aphid midges, lacewings, and ladybugs (or lady beetles), is an easy way to control aphids, and incredibly successful, though you may feel all the bugs are gone once you set them free. Don't be discouraged. Some will find other homes, but most will stay where the "food" is and remove these pesky insects from your plants. The natives are still in your garden - they are just better at hiding than the destructive ones are.

You can always use floating row covers if your crops are being devoured and you have treated the plants well first.

Caterpillars

If you see caterpillars on the leaves of your plants and bushes, try to identify them as best as possible - some of them become your garden Monarch or Tiger Lily butterflies. But most are, in fact, moths and of little benefit before or after developing wings.

Caterpillars have distinct head caps with six legs in the front and fleshy false legs in the back segments. They are most prevalent on shade trees, ornamentals, and vegetables, chewing on leaves or leaf edges. Many also tunnel into fruits and fleshy plant buds.

Again, introduce native predators and parasites if you can't see any in your garden in early spring. Floating row covers work well. Make sure you keep a close eye out when harvesting. Caterpillars are full-season pests and can be found in the spring, mid-summer, and fall.

Flea Beetles

These ravenous beetles are small, dark, and usually "jump" if you disturb them. They eat round holes in leaves, with a preference for young plants, while the larvae attack plant roots. Most vegetable crops can suffer from these creatures, so keep an eye out on all your plants.

Use floating row covers, or mix a batch of garlic stray (one-quart water with one teaspoon garlic oil) or kaolin clay (a soft white or pink clay) with the top ½ inch of soil around infested plants.

Slugs and Snails

Snails come out at night. Since they are night heathens, you rarely notice you have them until they have devastated a plant or you see their slightly iridescent trail on rocks, cement, or pavers. They hide under large-leaved plants, yard debris, mulched straw, or ground covers - anywhere they can have a respite from the sun, without being vulnerable to predators (birds). Then at night, they sneak out and eat holes in anything they can reach, from iris leaves to hostas and cabbage heads to lettuce. If it's green, they will eat it.

Many home remedies have been concocted to trap snails. Some gardeners go out at night with a flashlight and heavy-soled shoes. Others swear by putting a shallow dish of beer where they've been spotted. Snail bait is effective but extremely toxic to animals and children. This is, again, a good situation to check about with your local extension service and find out what has been successful in the current season.

Colorado Potato Beetle

Adult Colorado potato beetles are golden orange and have yellow and black striped, rounded wing covers. They are small, about ¼ of an inch long, with antennae and rust-colored legs. You will see them on your tomato plants,

eggplants, and petunias. They can be devastating to young plants, defoliating them quickly.

Controls include using straw mulch at the base of plants and throughout your box, spraying with neem oil, applying floating row covers, and hand picking them off plants. Native parasites and predators are good at controlling these pests too.

Cabbage Maggot

These larvae keep to the vegetables in the cabbage family, such as Brussel sprouts and all cabbages, especially Chinese cabbage. Maggots tunnel into your plants' roots, so you can usually detect them when plants die or are overtaken by other disease organisms.

Floating row covers work here also, but you can set squares of tar paper around newly transplanted sprouts. Cut slits in squares large enough to cover the root zone or leaf line - make sure plants are still receiving water easily.

Keep your planting to the later part of spring.

Mounding wood ash or red pepper dust at the base of your plants also keeps these maggots at bay. You can also apply parasitic nematodes around the roots, but don't use both the wood ash/pepper dust and nematodes. Either is fine, as with the former you may be killing the nematodes along with the maggots.

Cutworms

These worms are fat, about 1 inch long, and can be gray or black larvae. You may be able to find them just under the soil surface curled into a spiral during the day. However, because they are night-active, that is the best time to look for them.

They love early, young seedlings and chew through plant stems at ground level. They can devour a crop completely in a few days throughout the late spring and early summer months.

Discourage cutworms with "collars" on new plants, and hold off on planting until as late as possible in your season.

Tarnished Plant Bug

If you've spotted the fast-moving, mottled green or brown bugs in your garden, take note and move fast yourself. You can most often find them on the flowers of vegetable plants, sucking juices and causing leaf and fruit distortion, but you will also see their destruction on other kinds of fruits and plant foliage.

Adult bugs and nymphs are heathens to a garden and are also known for causing plant wilting, growth stunting, and tip dieback.

You can best manage these by keeping your raised bed weed-free, especially in the spring. Spray neem oil on the young nymphs in the spring, and encourage native predatory insect and row covers to continue their attack on these devastating bugs.

Scales

All three forms of these creatures are bad. Adult females appear as bumps on stems, leaves, or fruit. Males are tiny flying insects, and the larvae are very small, soft insects, crawling on plants with threadlike mouthparts. You will find scales on fruits, ornamental shrubs, trees, and even indoor plants. All forms of this insect suck plant sap, excreting a sticky substance on leaves and plant parts. Your plants will become yellow and drop leaves, or perhaps even die before you see these creatures, so investigate thoroughly. The sticky sap is the most obvious clue.

Control them by trimming damaged plant parts from healthy stems and leaves. Bring in native predators, and apply dormant or summer oil sprays to help maintain control throughout the season. Neem oil also works well. If you are still having trouble ridding your garden of scales, you can gently scrub them from the twigs with a soft brush and soapy water. Be sure to rinse your plants well afterward.

Japanese Beetles

Little ½ inch metallic blue-black beetles with a black iridescent skull cap and red wing covers, these beasts can devour a plant or flower in just a day, cutting holes into the leaves. Not only are the adult beetles a menace, but the larvae feed on lawn and garden plant roots too.

They have also been known to attack small fruits, such as grapes and cherries.

Control of these pests includes setting out baited traps upwind of your beds, on two sides, at least 30 feet from your plants. Different regions have different precautions, especially for organic baits, so check with your local extension service or garden supply nursery for the best solutions for your area. Having the two separate locations will give good coverage, as the beetles are also a bit wary of new items. Of course, floating row covers and insecticidal soap work too, and when spraying, don't be afraid to drown the beetle in liquid!

Mexican Bean Beetle

You may think you have a few discolored ladybugs, but don't be fooled - what you are seeing are Mexican Bean Beetles. About the same size and roundness as ladybugs, these beetles are yellow-orange and have 12 black spots on their wing covers.

The larvae are fat, dark yellow grubs with long branched spines and can be found with the adults on lima beans, snap beans, and soybeans. Adults cause leaves to have a lacy appearance by chewing on the green, fleshy parts.

They can be eliminated by planting early in the season and using floating row covers, so plants are established before any sign of the beetles appear. Insecticidal soap or neem oil also works. If you can lure spined soldier bugs to your yard, either the adults, which look like little flat tanks, or their yellow "spinely" larvae, you will be getting one of the most beneficial predators of these pesky bugs in your garden. You can buy them or spread pheromones.

Grasshoppers and Locusts

More often than not, if you have these insects in your area, you already have a pretty good idea of how to get rid of them - isolate and destroy! The younger you find them, the less chance there is of dealing with them in the next season.

These ravenous insects can destroy a plant in an afternoon, and if you have three or four chomping on it, they will take it to the ground. I've seen insecticides for these, and frankly, short of a blow-torch, all that will happen is contamination of your bed with poisons.

Something to be aware of, however, whether you are dealing with grasshoppers (which, literally, hop, and have over 40 species) or locusts (these fly and are a sub-species of their own), make sure you have heavy-soled shoes to step on them with. If you only "damage" them, they can hop away, hide, and give you lots of opportunities to be searching for descendants next season.

Beneficial Insects

Most of the time, when we speak about insects in the garden, we think of the pests that destroy our prized plants. However, there are just as many beneficial insects to help curb the infestations and havoc the awful insects cause. Let's discuss the ones you want, as well as how to attract and keep them in your garden.

Aphid Midge

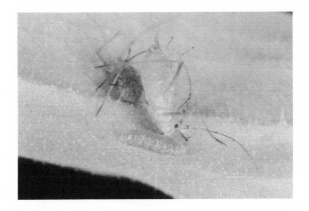

Planting many pollen plants will attract these transparent larvae, as well as the long-legged adult flies, to your yard. As the name suggests, these insects feed on more than 60 species of aphids,

keeping buds and new shoots clear of aphid infestations. Pollen plants are wide in variety, and the ones most beneficial for aphid midges will be the same plants that attract honey bees and butterflies.

Ground Beetles

If you are plagued by slugs and snails, your best beneficial insect defense is the ground beetle. Because they feed at night when snails and slugs are most active, they can be of huge benefit in combating the sly and shade-loving opposition. They also prey on cutworms and cabbage maggots. Planting a few perennials among your annual crops will provide them with a stable habitat, making them more willing to stay in your raised beds and gardens.

Braconid Wasps

There are several species of braconid wasps, and their markings vary from region to region. Check with your local extension service or nursery to find the markings of your region's preferred species. Female braconid wasps lay their eggs into a host caterpillar, moth, aphid, or beetle larvae, which, in turn, provides the larvae with food and nourishment. Upon the death of the host, the larvae have completed development and become wasps. Having an ample supply of nectar plants with small flowers, including wild carrot, yarrow, and dill, will help you attract the adults to your garden.

Lacewings

Planting angelica, cosmos, sweet alyssum, and coreopsis in your yard will attract lacewings, which feed on aphids, thrips, whiteflies, mealybugs, scales, and caterpillars. Adult lacewings and their larvae feed upon these predators, keeping your plants healthy and thriving.

You can also purchase them at nurseries and farmer association co-ops.

Damsel Bugs

Damsel bugs are used on alfalfa fields to control many types of damaging insects, including small caterpillars, leafhoppers, and aphids. You can use large nets to gather them from these fields and redistribute them to your own yard to control vegetable-damaging insects easily, or purchase them at local nurseries and gardening centers.

Minute Pirate Bugs

Though these bugs are small, they will attack just about any insect that moves and be very thorough in the destruction of it. Their brown and gold bodies and tan-colored legs move fast. Plant goldenrod, daisies, yarrow, and alfalfa to attract these beneficial bugs.

Lady Beetles (ladybugs)

I am very fond of these insects, whether adults, red with black spots, or in larvae form, which look like little charcoal-colored dragons. Both can be seen on a rosebud, chomping away on aphids, or randomly scattered throughout your yard. Either life form will help rid your garden of aphids, mealybugs, mites, and other sap-sucking insects. Plant coreopsis, dill, fennel, angelica, and yarrow to have ladybugs call your yard "home."

Soldier Beetles

Aphids and caterpillars fall victim to these beetles, although soldier beetles are not picky. These small, skinny beetles, ¼ to inch long, have black iridescent wing covers with a bright red head and are attracted to catnip, hydrangea, and goldenrod.

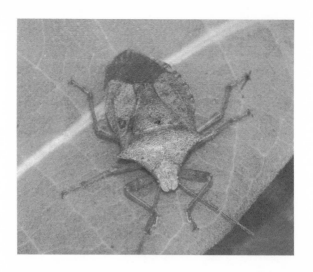

Spined Soldier Bug

Not to be confused with the pesky *stink bug*, soldier bugs are roundish bugs with distinctive *"pointed shoulders"* behind their head. They appreciate perennials for shelter and feed on beetle larvae and hairless caterpillars.

Tachinid Flies

Tachinid fly larvae, easily identified by their red eyes and yellowish bodies, will attack and burrow into many types of caterpillars, feeding on their host from the inside out. They are attracted to sweet clover, parsley, and dill, among other herbs, which provide food for the adults.

Fungus, Molds, and Rot

Fungi begin from other areas within a small distance of your plants. They are self-borne diseases, and most often, you don't even know you have them until it begins rotting your crops or causing the leaves of your plants to discolor and fall off. They are hard to get rid of and can continue to devastate a bed for seasons.

Fungi can hide in soil for ages. They seem to survive frost, frozen ground, heated droughts, and other extreme (and not so extreme) conditions. Though some fungi benefit the soil by breaking down organic matter quickly, others will rob you of your hard work and dedication with hardly any signs aside from your dying plants.

Common fungi can include most wild mushrooms (many are poisonous and should be removed with gloves), root rot, stem, collar, crown rots, wilt disease, and damping-off disease. Some wait for the plant to mature while others attack when they are seedlings.

If you suspect you have fungus, mold, or rot, take a soil sample to your local cooperative extension service and have them test your soil. It's free, and you will have an answer on which you can count. It may not save your current crop, but having answers will save your future plantings and harvests.

If you have fungus, mold, or rot, there are several things you can do to rid yourself of this attack.

- Get rid of all sick plants. Once you have a garden infestation, there is little you can do for the season. Getting rid of the infected plants is your first step. Do not put these plants in compost heaps or containers. The deceased plants should go directly into a waste bin and be disposed of.

- Clean up all current garden and yard debris, and again at the end of the season, so it can't provide a safe haven for future fungus. Again, throw it away; don't put it in a compost pile. Doing so will guarantee even more fungus and rot to deal with next season.

- Move your crops to new areas. Put the tomatoes where you had beans, move your herbs to where you had zinnias. Additionally, if you want to be really done with the fungus once and for all, plant your next season's plants in sterilized containers with new soil. Turn the soil in your beds every two weeks to keep it aerated and absent of excess moisture. Resting your beds for a few seasons will starve the fungus from plants to feed on and, thereby, kill it.

- Plant disease-resistant varieties of vegetables or bloomers. These hardy varieties are genetically stronger and have more tolerance to diseases and air-borne organisms.

- If you believe you may be susceptible to fungus or rot, check with your extension service and see if there are any fungicides that you can apply to prevent your beds from infestations.

They may offer organic solutions to help surviving beds recuperate from an attack.

- Lastly, if you still suspect the presence of fungus or rot after you've cleared out the affected plants and debris and rested it for a year or two, replace the soil. It is a hassle, for sure, but it is better than seeing all your nurtured plants fall to the menace of fungus once again.

Rodents

I'm going to go as far as deer on this one, as most of what they enjoy can also be enjoyed by smaller and just as voracious critters.

Voles, groundhogs, moles, and gophers are all fond of your garden plants, from the small tender shoots of your newly sprung peas to the expansive root system of a mature shrub. Having raised beds, especially elevated ones, will deter them from choosing your plant as an easy target, but these varmints will somehow find a way to chew on your beloveds the minute you turn your back.

Though many traps, poisons, and such are available, I've found that our local Wildlife and Game Service provides the best alternative to capturing rodents if deterring them from your plants isn't an answer. They set the traps, and all you have to do is call them when the trap is triggered. They then redistribute the animal to a more suitable location. Professional exterminators can also rid you of colonies, but most often, they exterminate the animal, and I'm not a big fan of that method or the poisons.

The traps and poisons you can buy at a home center are expensive and rarely work, though some have had success. I do not recommend these methods in any case.

Preventative maintenance can also be a good deterrent. If these animals feel there is no way to get to the food, they may find other places for their meals. Surround your boxes with wide wire fencing, or mount "eaves" on the tops of taller boxes, angled outward, so the animal can't get up and over.

I've also heard cats are a great deterrent but if there were a chance of raccoons in the area, I wouldn't risk my pet for a fight among the brave! Cage-eaves over boxes work the best, and if on a hinge, will easily maintain your plants and keep out unwanted critters.

Pets and Children

In all my years of gardening, I have never had to worry about my kids getting into the garden unless it was to "harvest the crops" early without my knowledge - this was a common occurrence in our raspberry patch!

I had gardened with my kids since they were toddlers, so they have respect for small plants and tiny seedlings. They even had their own barrel filled with whatever plants they chose at the garden center. One year we had purple radishes, purple cabbages, and purple beets!

The dogs, on the other hand, had no reason to stay out of the soft, cool dirt that surrounded the plants. I'm sure cats also believe the ground under a productive tomato plant does nicely as a naptime spot as well as a litter box.

Several methods have worked for me to deter pets, from fencing the beds off completely to sticking plastic forks, handle side down, in the dirt just enough to "poke" their feet if they step in the bed. Of course, there is always the "Hey, get out of there!" yell that not only warns the animals but spooks too!

Traffic

Many people are now putting raised beds on the strips of land between their front sidewalk and the street - what I refer to as a "hell strip." These areas, also known as a road verge, are often a wasteland of ground, harboring every known weed to humanity, rocks, gravel, snowmelt and salt, neighborhood leaves, trash, and who knows what else might be blown from the road or gutter into your yard.

By segmenting off raised boxes, however, you can raise the ground level up a few more inches higher than the collective. You will have control over the irrigation of lawns or plants while making the area an appealing and inviting place.

Try putting rocks or gravel at ground level and then raising the plants in boxes, some with shrubs, perennials, tomatoes, or berries. That way, you can create a very appealing design while also taking advantage of extra space.

If you plant hedge shrubs, such as arborvitae, you will also create a sound buffer to your yard. Trees would also benefit by having a raised bed protection, giving them direct water, protection from hazards while young, and color for annuals when mature. Choose small trees that don't need a huge area for their root system. Anything growing over 10 feet tall would be too large to thrive in a "hell strip" and would suffer and die as soon as its roots' drip line reaches the road or the sidewalk.

Anything you decide to put in your raised bed would benefit from protection, be it vegetables, garden plants, a living fence, or trees. Be creative and explore the possibilities of having more room!

Chapter Summary

- The use of beneficial insects coupled with good garden practices will keep your raised bed free from infestations and pest damage.
- Keeping a close eye on your plants will give you the advantage of proactive, diligent maintenance of a productive garden.

In the next chapter, you will learn the secrets for productive, repetitive, and successful planting practices.

5

VEGETABLES, PERENNIALS, VINES, AND SHRUBS

There are a number of advantageous ways you can increase your harvest, health of plants and shrubs, or sturdiness of blooms in your raised beds. By using just a few specific techniques, you can be a garden expert and have a beautifully successful garden to prove it!

Vegetables - Think Outside the Square

For maximum food harvest and garden interest, group your varieties in triangles instead of rows or squares. Working with the angle means you will be able to plant approximately 5% to 15% more plants in the same area as opposed to a more defined pattern. Grouping your plants will help you to create a diverse garden bed, giving bees and other natural pollinators better access to varietal pollination while creating visual aesthetics for yourself. Keep the spacing according to package or planting suggestions, while considering the planting area as a triangle instead of a square.

Go Vertical

The other day, I was driving to my dad's house and noticed his neighbor, who always has prized melons, with the vines going around his chain-link fence. He was making use of the vertical sunshine at the back of the bed, giving him more room in front of the melons to plant tomatoes and peppers. Ingenious!

If you don't have a fence, create a series of stakes or build a grid or trellis staked into the ground, to support zucchini or other prolific creeping vines. These are wonderfully adverse vegetables to grow but take up every inch of dirt their tendrils can reach. Trellis and fence sections can also work well for training blooming plants and vines and creating a mixed-interest garden.

Creeping plant varieties, such as roses, honeysuckle, clematis, cucumbers, squash, peas, and beans, can also benefit from growing skyward. Make sure you stake the canes or vines securely, as well as any crops during the growing season. The stems will develop stronger and thicker as the melon or banana squash grows. I always value the "better safe than sorry" notion. So, it won't do me any good to go to the trouble of staking a cantaloupe vine if I don't secure a net below the growing fruit!

While vertically attaching stems gives the plant more space and air and reduces access to ground prowling insects and fungus, you will also be making your life as the gardener easier. Maintenance is easier and takes less time, as will harvesting your crops, since you will be aware of where your vegetables and melons are developing.

Pairing Plants in a Raised Bed

Due to the close proximity within a raised bed, it would be to your plants' benefit to design your beds for the best outcome. Not only will this make for healthier plants today, but it will give your soil the rest it needs from one crop to another, as each one pulls different nutrients from the soil. Phosphate-loving potatoes pair well with nitrogen-loving tomatoes, for example.

Also, it is a wise and respectful gardener who listens to the experience of Native American traditions - plant with the "3 Sisters."

- Corn, beans, and squash *"Sturdy cornstalks support the beans, while squash grows on the ground, keeping out weeds and shading the soil to lessen water evaporation and increase root growth."*

More advantageous vegetable combinations include -

- Tomatoes, basil, and onions
- Leaf Lettuce and brassicas or peas
- Carrots, onions, and radishes
- Beets and celery

Succession Planting

Planting certain crops at certain times means you can get several harvests or bloom periods from one plot of ground. Think of the natural cycle of bulbs blooming first in the garden, flowering bushes bursting with color next, perennials picking up the next splash of color throughout summer, and fall chrysanthemums and ornamental cabbages just before the snow melts.

Just as nature provides us with all these blooming cycles, so can your raised bed provide you with multiple harvests of fruits and vegetables, as well as blooming annuals, rose cuttings, and perennial seedlings.

Begin your beds with lettuces, perhaps early-maturing corn, a second planting of warm-weather lettuces with garlic and onions intermingled, and then a twining cucumber or two to finish out the bounty.

Or asparagus, followed by beans, cherry tomatoes, and potatoes.

Or, revert to early English gardening with iris, clematis, foxgloves, and daisies for a continual season of blooms.

Get the best results from this rotating garden by adopting a few of these secrets -

- Use potted seedlings or container plants, and set them in your boxes when the risk of frost has passed. This will give you a head start on the season and a faster first-crop harvest.
- Choose the "early" varieties of the crops you want to have. These varieties usually produce smaller vegetables or fruits but taste just as wonderful with, more than likely, a higher quantity of harvest.
- In between plantings, supplement your soil with more compost and work it into the top few inches of soil. This will replenish the used nutrients giving your next crop the benefit of a newly planted bed.
- Cover your beds with floating row covers,

water walls, cloches, or other plant protectors to begin your season even earlier.

While we are talking about protection and keeping your plants healthy and safe, let's further discuss environmental hazards, such as frost, snow, winds, and cold snaps.

Protecting Your Plants

Many techniques have become common practice for seasoned gardeners when protecting their gardens. As we've talked about, having a raised bed garden is the ultimate way to give your plants every benefit imaginable. But what happens when events outside of your control threaten them, namely, Mother Nature?

Below are many of the tried and true methods used by professional and amateur gardeners alike, and while none is hands-down the best way to protect all your plants, many were devised centuries ago and still prove to be great choices today. Here are a few of the popular methods, along with the details you will need to know to make their use ideal.

Floating row covers - This light, breezy material is water penetrable but is still able to keep frost off your plants. Using this technique can save your new seedlings in the spring while also extending your season in the fall. And as you've read, this material will also protect young seedlings and buds from devastating insects.

Stable row covers - I've seen quite a few different takes on this, from pinned-down clear fiberglass roof panels to heavy clear plastic spread over supports and more.

You are keeping out the cold but maintaining air circulation, so monitor these types of protection, as they can get very hot if not well-ventilated. They are wonderful to invest in if you plan on having multiple seasons of raised beds, early or late season gardening, or want to extend your seasons. They are also easy to store when you aren't using them.

Cloches - This technique began in the Middle Ages and is still used prolifically today. Clear vessels with a large opening at the bottom are placed over young seedlings to protect from the frost while also creating a small "hothouse" where each plant can thrive. A clear liter plastic bottle with the bottom cut off also serves the purpose well and provides its own ventilating system when you remove the cap.

Water-walls - These vinyl "walls" are actually thin tubes of plastic attached together, which are stood around a plant. These are most often advertised for use with tomatoes, but any plant can benefit from their protective yet breathable environment. The "tubes" are then filled with water, which keeps the air inside the wall at an even temperature. The tubes have too much water to freeze, while still being able to raise the heat within.

Cold frames - This is a type of cover you'd put over your boxes to keep the wind and cold out, but let the light in. Often, they are a plastic or glass "window" of sorts, which is hinged to the back or side of the box and opened or closed when the need arises. Using clear plastic, 6 mils or thicker, will give strength, be cost-effective, and protect plants from spring and fall elements when affixed to a frame - although any clear, stable material can be used, such as acrylic or glass. Make sure the frame is sturdy, so you won't have to worry about broken glass in the soil or snow collapsing their frames.

Let's Plant!

Whether you are starting your plants from seed, cuttings, seedlings, or containers, such as flats or pots, your plants will love being in a raised bed. For your plants, it's comparable to staying in a 5-star hotel. But it's still good to know what type of plants do better from what kind of starts.

When determining the size and growth cycle you want to begin your beds at, take these considerations into account -

The Length of Your Locations' Growing Season

If you have a particularly long growing season, say from mid-February to late November, you may not be concerned with a shorter growing season or needing short-season producing plants.

If, however, you are looking to extend your season as much as possible with seeds, starting them early inside to transplant into your raised bed will give you a head start on a short season. If your plants begin to really take off, you may have to move them to larger containers before putting them outside, but growth in a healthy seedling is rarely hindered by the extra time it may take to move it to a larger "home."

There is also a certain satisfaction in growing your plants from seed. You probably already understand this since you are reading this book. The plants become an investment, and anything we have a personal investment in is a benefit to not only our pantries but also our well-being.

One last consideration: by starting your raised beds from seeds, you also have a larger variety of choices for the types of crops you want. The garden centers mostly carry the general, hardy varieties, which give them the best revenue. You will find a bit more variety at a nursery, but again, they are looking to satisfy the general public, not the gardener who strives for unique and unusual plantings.

If you are an adventurer, you may want to try your hand at tri-color clematis, purple string beans, or heirloom tomatoes. Online seed catalogs and well-established seed farms have wonderful new cultivars to try also, which bring another level of anticipation to gardening in your own yard.

Expected First-harvest Crop

In areas that have a short growing period, especially for plants that have a long period until harvest - for example, melons, most corn, large squash, or pumpkins - you may want to start with container plants to shorten the time until your first harvest. Another consideration should also include the variety's ability to mature quickly. If you choose a variety that has a first crop production time of 120 days, it could be a factor for choosing the type of plants you want to have in your beds.

Transplanting from Your Raised Beds (Annuals and Young Cuttings)

Many gardeners use raised bed gardening as a "holding" or "staging" area for plants they want to transplant into their landscape and yards when their areas are ready after a landscaping redesign or new sprinkler installation. If this is your plan, you probably have a pretty good idea of when you want to transplant from your raised beds.

In such a case, then schedule backward, and figure when you can put your seeds or plants into the raised beds without the risk of frost.

Then, approximate as closely as you can when you could put the maturing plants into your raised bed. You won't want to transplant growing seedlings and cuttings too soon, but you also don't want to overshoot the planting season and transplant when the weather is too warm.

Example -

If you want to have pumpkins ready to pick at the beginning of October, and the Striped Golden Globe has a 120-day period from plant to harvest time, you will want to aim for early July to set new blossoms. It may take 30 to 40 days for the plant to be mature enough to set blossoms. This puts you at mid-May to have seedlings in the raised bed. And remember, these aren't seeds - they are seedlings or sturdy plants which will begin growing to a mature, fully producing plant within a month.

Trying to out-maneuver Mother Nature is a tricky business, but your plants will greatly appreciate any small benefit you can provide to deter the elements and extend their growing season.

Vegetables

Seeds - As I mentioned before, starting your garden from seed can be time-consuming, but it can also be economical and give you a larger choice of varieties to propagate in your garden.

When starting seeds, pick "containers" that can be transplanted directly into the ground. I have found the small pellet-type pods to have a supposedly disintegrating net within them but have yet to see one "disintegrate" after I planted it. Judge for yourself, but I've found these to constrict roots once they begin to grow and fill the raised bed.

I've used ice cream cones, the light, airy ones, not the waffle-type cone. These cones, I have found, disintegrate well while still keeping their shape throughout the growing period. Once in the ground, they dissolve easily. Because the cone is made from organic material, it *may* (don't quote me on this!) contribute to some sort of feeding. I haven't done a side-by-side test; I just know they hold together long enough for the seed to sprout, grow to seedling size, and transplant easily. And my dogs can't seek them out to nibble on them after I've planted them.

Other types of seed containers can range from cardboard egg cartons to ice cube trays with a hole punched in the bottom for drainage. Whatever your choice, give it a shot and see how it goes. If they don't take off, you haven't lost much of anything, aside from your time and the cost of the seeds. And maybe a bit of disappointment. But if they grow and give you plants, then the green of your thumb just grew to a darker shade of green!

Containers - If you aren't too particular to the variety of vegetables you grow, container plants progress well and develop quickly, as they are usually planted with a time-release feeding product and have the right type of soil for whatever vegetable is being grown. They are most often tried and true producers for a greater success rate and will give you a productive garden box, whether you are growing ornamentals or vegetables and fruits.

When moving these plants into your raised bed, you may want to consider a few points:

- Purchase plants early to get the best choice of health and variety.
- Consider the weather and your means of protection, if needed, when transplanting into the raised bed.
- Stake, fence, or trellis appropriately *before* planting, so when the plant is in, it will only have the task of growing strong and producing abundantly. Trying to side-step young plants to erect appropriate support systems for mid to full-season growth is tempting the gardening

gods. Inevitably, you will end up stepping on one plant while avoiding another.

Propagating - If you are starting vegetables or cuttings from previous crops, such as potatoes, lavender, or onions, begin these indoors and move outside when root systems show support for the plant, as well as a guarantee of warm weather conditions. Cuttings and propagation are a tried and true way of producing healthy plants for your beds, and sometimes when you have a great strain of particularly tasty golden potatoes or green onions, it's hard not to give it a try. We've all grown an avocado seed, right? Well, take this process a step or two further and see if you can get your own cuttings, or that of a fellow gardener, sprouted and ready for your raised bed!

Annuals

With flowering annuals and the thought of only being able to enjoy their blooms for one season, it is hard to spend tens, if not hundreds, of dollars on them. There are some alternatives, and I believe your mind is already a few steps ahead of me in devising ways to create your own sprouted container, flower box, or raised bed full of color.

Seeds - As with vegetables, make sure your containers will transplant into soil easily. Stay away from the "peat pellets" and use a more organic form of container. Keep in mind, the goal when transplanting seedlings is to not disturb the tender, new roots that have formed when you are able to move them outside. Doing so will undo all the effort and care you've given the seeds up to this point.

Use a common ice cream cone (*not* the waffle kind) or another similar type of organic vessel that will disappear when planted in the ground. Some gardeners have even used eggshells.

I have a story in relation to using eggshells. One spring, I decided to use the compost I had been "growing" for a few seasons. It looked rich and robust, and I was anxious to see how my plants would do in the organic mulch I had created. It began with some extra potting soil I had, supplementing it with kitchen scraps and organic greens.

After tilling a bed for planting, I spread the compost around and gently raked it into the top inch of the soil. No more than five minutes later, I found my Labrador digging and snooping around in the dirt, vacuuming up clumps of the organic material. After a closer look, I discovered he was digging out the eggshells, which I realized I hadn't crushed into small enough pieces.

So... if you use eggshells, you may want to break the shells and slide the seedlings gently out before planting, because as good as eggshells may be for aerating the soil, they also are a great fiber source for canines who like a tasty clump of dirt!

Starts - I've seen gardeners successful with using starts for annual flowers, but most of the time, it is in temperate climates with little downtime from cutting to planting in a bed or garden. Pelargoniums (common geraniums), hydrangeas, and roses come to mind. Consider, though, in these mild climates, pelargoniums and the like aren't annuals - they return easily year after year. Where I live, they are annuals, and don't do well if I try to propagate with cuttings. If you have distinctive three to four seasons, you may want to try these when the weather is cold outside - experimenting is always fun. And what a treat it would be to have a winter-grown start, root-out, and bloom the following June!

Containers - As mentioned earlier, these are the most expensive way to put color into your garden but most often, and especially if you live in a shorter growing season, having the plants already started and close to blooming is a wonderful event. Pick plants that are on the verge of explosion, but have plenty of room for growth. Don't pick the largest plant just because it seems to be the strongest. Quite often, annuals can be pot-bound, and if the plant looks like it is just a bit too big for its container, find one that is smaller. Root-bound plants have constrained roots and won't absorb nutrients or water with the vigor that's needed to support a large plant, even if you try to spread the roots out when you plant them. The roots have been able to absorb water from the congregated moisture in the pot, but when put into the dirt, this will dissipate, and your plant will die. If you pick a smaller yet healthy and lively plant, it will reach out to get what it needs instead of fighting itself for survival.

Perennials

These are my favorite type of plant, whether vegetables, bloomers, shrubs, or vines. First, because I don't have to plant or have any thought about what I should do each season, other than clear away the debris from fall winds. Second, because each growing season gives them more time to build from where they left off the summer before.

They seem to thrive and increase in size without much help from me. As long as I water, apply food ever so often, and keep pests at bay, these strong and vigorous plants supply me with blooms, color, crops, and landscape beauty year upon year upon year.

Perennial vegetables and fruits can include many types of berries (canes as well as creepers, such as raspberries and strawberries), asparagus, rhubarb, and onions. Perennial flowers and shrubs number more than I can mention here but include lavender, roses, clematis, and potentilla. Whatever your desire, it would be hard not to find a perennial that could satisfy your wants.

Seeds - Buying perennial seeds is a wonderful way to try new varieties and substantiate older beds that might be thinning out. Many of the more prevalent perennials can be found and also offer new colors, different heights, and specific tolerances for particular environments or zones. Some of my favorite perennials to watch for each season include hollyhocks, foxglove (all parts of which are poisonous, so keep them far from pets and children), poppies, yarrow, wildflowers, California poppy, and morning glory. Be sure to leave several seed pods on the last of season bloomers to replenish your beds for next season.

Starts - Beginning a perennial by cutting works well, but some do it with less fuss than others. While some take hold from woodier stems of their parent plants, others may benefit from a nice young shoot. Do your homework on the ones you love and see if you have any local garden clubs or neighbors who can share their success and tricks to root out cuttings successfully.

When I was younger, I remember my mother using cuttings from her father's garden, as well as friends and neighbor gardeners. Additionally, search online to see how gardeners propagate starts, particularly for hydrangeas and roses, to get a jump-start on several beneficial routines and the latest techniques.

Containers - While this is likely the most expensive way to have perennials in your beds, boxes, and containers, it is by no means a wasted effort of cash. If I were to commit to a preferred way of planting new beds, I would have to say containers are my favorite.

Plants are vigorous, and most often, transplanting is quite easy.

Though I do have to save my pennies during the year for my spring splurge, in my circumstance, I save money in the long run. I have dogs, so by giving the plants the extra benefit of being "noticed" because of their larger size, they are less likely to be trodden upon after planting. Also, I know I buy a variety that has been tested in gardens for a few seasons and is of a stronger strain. I also like the thought of seeing bloom or crops on a first season plant, as opposed to waiting for a year for seedlings or cuttings to take hold. Call me impatient, but that's just how I like it,

Containers also offer a few different varieties, though they may not be the years' new hybrids. They all come with the directions for each plant (the same facts that you will see on the back of a seed packet). I can plan my design on the fly, even at the nursery, as opposed to scouring catalogs and the internet (though I could hardly call this an arduous task). If I haven't taken the time to scout out the nurseries' plants online, doing so at the point of purchase works just fine also.

Other types of perennial plants you will see in your readings include -

Corms, tubers, rhizomes, and bulbs - Dahlias, camellias, peonies, gladiolas, and azaleas - in four-season areas, some of these are considered annuals, as they don't survive winter temperatures, but in milder climates, they do go dormant for a bit to rejuvenate for a lovely next season of bloom and growth.

Iris, ferns, horseradish, and bamboo are rhizomes and lie at ground level or just below the soil surface. They propagate easily and should be "thinned" every four to five years or when the plants begin to grow on top of themselves.

Bulbs, which are planted beneath the ground anywhere from three to 12 inches down, include tulips, hyacinths, crown imperials, and narcissus. Bulbs are planted the season before, so they receive a dormant "cold" period to stimulate growth when it warms. The varieties are endless and provide the earliest color and crops in your garden. And, once planted, you rarely have to do anything more than watering and clearing away spent foliage after the blooming season.

Vines

Vines come in many types and growth patterns, and while some are annuals, many are perennials too. You will also be able to find just about any vine for a harvest of goodies or a feast for the eyes. Whether you are planting a blooming variety or a crop producer, keep vines to the north, or the back of your raised beds, as they will climb the trellis and create dense shade for anything growing behind them.

Annual vines include several tropical varieties, which will more often than not be offered as container plants, such as bougainvillea or mandevilla. You can purchase these as a container plant to be brought in at the end of the season in colder climates. If you are looking to have the vines for only one season, consider morning glory or jasmine, offering beautiful blooms and enticing scents.

Perennial vines give us numerous reasons to think vertically in the garden, whether you are trellising sweet grapes or a beloved wisteria (use caution). In addition to grapes, many vines are known to produce wonderful blooms as well as fruit, such as honeyberry (related to honeysuckle). Perennial vines tend to be hearty, and in some locations, invasive, so do your research before putting in your vines.

Seeds - Annual vines are usually stated on their seed packets and are often planted directly into the bed where you'd like the vine to be. Some need to have their outer seed cover nicked, enabling the seedling to sprout quickly. I always buy a package of morning glory in the spring for my summer garden. The blue blooms are beautiful, and they always give me something to anticipate towards.

Starts - Most often, if you are thinking of putting a vine in as a start, you are thinking of a perennial. These include most varieties of grapes, trumpet vine, and climbing hydrangea. Because these types of plants are so hardy, taking a cutting and rooting it out is a very smart way to create a perennial foundation in your beds without little expense. They most often are easy to root out and will transplant well too. Be sure the vines you are considering are plants *you really want* because some are considered invasive in certain climates, particularly trumpet vines (the common varieties), ivies, and wisteria (if it isn't trellised well).

Containers - Once again, you will see many vines producing edibles and blooms in containers, and you will see them thriving. Since most harvest-producing vines take more than one season to become established, you may want to consider buying in a container to get a head start for same-year crop production. The same goes for blooming vines, but these tend to be a bit more temperamental. Some produce blooms in the first season; others can take one or two to become a specimen.

Shrubs and Trees

I've loved raised bed shrub fences for as long as I can remember. I'm not sure if it came from books with secret gardens or living mazes, but I am a long-time friend of raised bed hedges.

About six years ago, I began my quest for a living fence and had planted a raised bed of soft conifers to absorb noise while also providing me with a beautiful green hedge. I lost two in the first year because I assumed my irrigation was reaching all the shrubs. But, after some struggle, each shrub has doubled in size and gives me privacy beyond my hopes and dreams. Rightly so, I have supplied them with abundant food and care, so my 4-foot soldiers grew as quickly and strong as any shrubbery could possibly grow. I needed no permits, nor did I have to set concrete posts or worry about gates. They are a beautiful addition to my front yard.

Containers - I'm going to suggest buying container-grown shrubs and trees unless you are transplanting an already established, hardy plant. Beginning from a cutting is possible, and I've done it with tree peonies, but other shrubs have been unsuccessful, and I've tried my hardest under almost every type of circumstance I could. Due to the fact that shrubs and trees have an established root system, trying to get one from an already highly developed start (a cutting) demands incredible support. When begun from a stem, an unestablished root system isn't immediately available to supply the needed nutrients and water to the established stem. Aside from rose bush cuttings, shrubs and trees struggle when trying to begin a new life away from an established root ball.

When establishing shrubs and trees in a raised bed, the number one concern should be irrigation. Make sure your shrub or tree is watered fully, at least once a week. This gives the plant a reason to "go deep" to establish its main root system, developing a healthier, well-established, weather-resilient tree or shrub, which won't topple in a storm or be dependent on shallow, seasonal water. A deep root zone reaches groundwater and will also flourish below sprinkler and sewer lines that may crisscross a larger raised bed plant.

If you are looking to border your yard or raised bed, there are a few varieties that grow well side by side. Since you may be looking to protect the plants inside the box, soften noise, establish garden rooms, or create a formal border, you will want to pre-decide on how thick the established hedge would be, how tall you would like it to mature to (some may require seasonal trimming) and the denseness between branches (some will cut off light totally).

Many popular varieties include boxwoods for formal or smaller hedges, arborvitae and laurels for medium height hedges, and poplars and pines for large windbreaks and shade. Follow plant recommendations, or contact your local extension service, arborist, or nurseryman for suggestions on what varieties would be best for your preferred conditions.

Chapter Summary

- Whether you begin your plants by seed or purchase container-grown plants, calculating

the length of season and maturity time
determines success.

- Careful planning and design can give you
  double or triple your production.

In the next chapter, you will learn gardening tricks to lengthen your season and develop sturdy, well-producing roses.

6

A ROSE IS A ROSE

My heart still softens when I think of roses. A traditional bloom for centuries, roses conjure up old-fashioned cottage gardens and the delicate fragranced soap at grandma's house.

Whether you are thinking of climbing a rose over a boxed arbor or sectioning out prized grandifloras in a raised bed all to themselves, having roses in your garden will raise your spirits and your landscape appeal throughout the summer season when little else is blooming.

If you've contemplated mixing up your raised beds with bloomers and vegetables, consider a rose in the mix. Doing a bit of reading and selecting a perfectly sized rose for the area will help you find a complementary color and style to assimilate easily within your garden's raised bed scheme.

Though many believe roses to be high maintenance, I've found this statement to be far from the truth. True, they do appreciate a bit of care, but nothing much more than any other perennial or vegetable inhabitant of your box beds. The key is to start your rose off with good soil, and because it will be in a raised bed designed and constructed by yourself, it will reap all the benefits before you even begin thinking of its necessities.

Roses are very diverse in their habits. You can find roses that are:

- suited to partial shade
- disease-resistant
- miniature
- shrubs
- climbers
- grandiflora
- floribunda
- heirloom
- one-time bloomers
- ever-blooming

The list goes on and on. And whether you think you know anything about roses, or know nothing at all, by just having an appreciation for these sun-loving, heavy blooming perennials, you will be leaps and bounds ahead of other gardeners in your neighborhood.

Myths of Rose Care

I'd like to decipher a few misgivings straddled by roses.

Thorns - Yes, most have thorns, and some of them can be deadly! But some roses are thornless or have very small thorns, similar to soft-nubbed shrubs. If you are adamant about not having a plant with thorns, you can even find a thornless rose, and you won't have to search far for these. But before doing so, consider this: if you plant a rose that does have a few thorns, it won't take long for intruders, be they children, pets, or strangers to your garden, to understand there is a rose to be dealt with. And rarely will they rise to the challenge of overcoming it. Having a slightly thorny shrub close to your prize-winning strawberries may prove to be an advantageous and defensive game plan.

Pruning - Indeed, roses do benefit from pruning, especially the heavy bloomers. Because their 4" to 6" blooms weigh the stem, pruning out weak branches makes the remaining stems stronger and capable of supporting those huge blooms. There are also rose shrubs that don't need or benefit from pruning; these being shrub and moss roses, which can stand side by side like bushes to form a gorgeous hedge. Or consider ground cover roses, which creep no higher than 8", but yet give your beds' corner a beautiful carpet of colorful flowers.

Finicky - While many complain about the pickiness of a rose's needs, most often their requirements can be attributed to gardener errors. Whether a rose has been placed in an area unsuited to its genetics or it is trying to tolerate conditions it wasn't bred to endure, roses have had to suffer the mislabeling of being high-maintenance. Roses do have their share of pests and disease, but no more so than any other plant sharing space in your garden. If you are out tending to cucumbers, you won't spend any more time on a rose.

Because roses have been popular for so many centuries, there are volumes of facts, information, and suggestions on every rose type sold, from northern to southern continents. There are roses that thrive best in humid conditions, just as there are roses that do better in arid conditions. Some tolerate heat waves, while others only bloom once in the spring. As I mentioned at the beginning of this chapter, there is a rose for just about any condition Mother Nature can throw out. This gives you ample opportunity to find one, or many, well suited for your situation and preference.

By having a rose in your raised garden bed, you will complement not only the partnering nearby plants, but you will be adding a streak of beauty to satisfy your own aesthetical necessities too.

General Necessities of Roses

Roses, generally, like to have damp feet and lots of sun, but as I've said, these generalities have been genetically out-bred, giving way to offering a rose for any garden nuance.

Roses like to be fed, just like vegetables. A good, basic fertilizer, which feeds the roots as well as the blooms, will be appreciated and is best when given as an organic (also, just like your vegetables). Fish emulsion, Epsom salts, digging manure or guano into the surrounding soil are also beneficial to roses. Make sure the manure isn't too hot, as this can burn roots and damage your bush. Keep to an evenly balanced feeding, such as 10-10-10 (a fertilizer analysis of nitrogen, phosphorus, and potash for total plant-feeding)

- this will do the trick nicely and keep your rose producing blooms and thriving all season long.

Roses most often should be pruned in the fall but can also benefit from a quick trim in the spring to remove dead blooms, stems, and debris. Spring blooms come from established canes, so keep an eye on the green nubs and don't go too far down the stem.

Roses also benefit from a good spraying every so often, as well as depositing beneficial insects, like lady beetles (ladybugs) and lacewings. If you begin before you see any pests in your yard, all your plants will benefit from this care.

Since there are so many types of roses available for you to choose from, let us discuss some of the general differences so you have a basic idea of your many choices.

Types - Segmenting out a rose gets a bit convoluted, but let's give it a try. Roses are available as bushes, shrubs, climbers, ground covers, and specimen plants. After you've decided on what kind of shape and size you'd like your rose to be, you have multiple choices of the kind of bloom your rose will have.

They also are divided into groups, such as:

- floribunda - many blooms on a single stem, smaller flowers, and generally, more compact
- grandiflora - large blooms, singly on a stem, with classic form
- tea rose - smaller than grandifloras, with the

same basic characteristics of a single stem and
traditional form
- hybrid teas - prize-winning bushes, known for
specialty form, fragrance, color, and style, think
long-stemmed roses

You can also find:

- miniatures - smaller bushes with small blooms
in a floribunda style
- cabbage and damask roses - older style roses,
multi-petaled with a shrub form, most often
have incredible fragrance
- breeder styles - the most popular is probably
David Austin roses, densely petaled flowers of
smaller size than hybrid teas and more old-
fashioned in form
- moss roses - if a rose were wild, it would be this
style, with smaller thorns, softer form, and
more relaxed blooms

So, after all of that, if you are wondering if you could
find a miniature climber, the answer would be "yes." If
you wanted to explore ground covers in shades of pink
with a wonderful fragrance, you are likely to have many
to choose from there as well. The choices are endless!

Visual Placement - Because there are so many varieties and styles of roses, quite often, determining the size you have available for your rose is a good place to begin your quest.

Some shrub roses can reach 8' high and just as wide across. Others can climb the entire side of a cottage, while some varieties can take up no more room than a cat basking in the sun. Choose your location, make sure it's sunny, and measure it by square feet. Then you can begin to look at the types of blooms you love and decide if you'd like it to be a continuous bloomer (one large flush of blooms in the spring followed by a continuous smaller parade throughout the season), or a one-time bloomer (huge, magnificent borage of blooms in the spring).

Support - If you are getting a climbing rose, give yourself a wide place to tie rose canes to, which then bloom upward from the horizontal cane. Plan on approximately 4' to give you ample space as the "*trellisor.*" Giving your rose enough room to allow you to trellis and stake it will make your life much easier, especially if you choose a rose with a particularly thorny disposition.

Floribundas have many blooms on one stem and look like a perfect bouquet all by themselves. Because they can get a bit top-heavy, staking may help keep the canes from bending to the ground. You will not know this until you get it into your location, however, what may be sturdy in one zone, may easily lean in a windy spot. Because these bushes tend to have smaller canes, you may need to remove deadwood in the fall. Rest assured, the extra care you offer will give you a show in bloom rarely matched.

Hybrid teas and grandiflora roses can benefit from "staking" the canes, but if you prune well, your canes will be strong enough to hold themselves and their heavier blooms upright. These roses are most often what florists sell as long stem roses.

Cabbage, damask, and moss roses are habitually shrub roses, and I think of their needs as something between lilacs and forsythias. In other words, you can stake, prune, or let them run amok, and the bush will still look beautiful and lush. Keep a close eye on the description of the particular rose you are contemplating and judge accordingly.

Pruning - If you spoke to five different rose experts about how they prune roses, you'd get six different answers on how to do it. However, there are some basic things to keep in mind, like pruning out dead wood as far down as you can, sealing cuts with paraffin or a tack (if you have rose bores), and deadheading blooms to the first 5-leaf stem. The angle of your cut can also determine which direction your rose stem will grow - a more horizontal cut with the ground will produce growth from the top, and a more vertical cut will produce growth from the side - to how far back you should prune to stimulate new growth.

Two things I make sure of each time I begin pruning:

1 - My hand-pruners are sharp and well oiled

2 - I have long sleeves or cuffed gloves on while doing it

As I said earlier, roses are very forgiving - a mistake in pruning here or there won't kill your bush. As long as you are timely in feeding it great fertilizer and making sure it gets lots of sun, your rose will give you the tolerance you need until you become a rose expert - which may take you all of one season, at the most!

Pests and Diseases

There are a few specific bugs and diseases that can devastate a rose, no matter what kind or how tolerant it is. Here are the main ones:

Aphids - As mentioned earlier, aphids suck sap from the stems and bloom hips of your rose. A good forceful spray with the hose can get them off, but keeping them off is the key to maintaining rose health. When I see them appear, as I do every spring, I mix an insecticidal soap: one teaspoon of dish soap (Dawn seems to work best) with two cups of water. I spray this on the bugs until they fall off, so if they haven't drowned, hopefully, the soap will take care of the rest. Then I bring in the big guns - *ladybugs* (or lacewings depending on your locality and time of year). These little powerhouses go to town on all my bushes, and when they seem to have finished, they lay their eggs, and their larva (little charcoal colored Gila monster-looking bugs with slender bodies and a couple of small red markings - see the section on Beneficial Insects) keep them out the rest of the season.

Rose bores - If you see holes in the pruned stems of your roses, you have rose bores. As adults, they look like small flies and hover around your bushes in groups of two to three. They lay their eggs in the stems after "boring" into the exposed soft flesh of your rose. Preventative measures are the only way I've found to combat these devils, and I have used many methods over the years. At first, I used white glue, which when dabbed on the top of a fresh cut, seemed to do the trick. By the time the glue had dissolved due to weather, the stem had hardened off to where the bores couldn't penetrate the cane. My mom used thumbtacks, which are more permanent and stay in the stem better, but I found that I kept running out of them, as rose borers also attack raspberries, and I had a raised bed the size of 18' X 20' full of them.

There are also "treatments" you can purchase at nurseries if you are in a location where these bugs are prevalent, but I never had much success with them. They are mostly systemic treatments, which means you mix the product with water and pour it around the base of the plant or directly on the bush itself. The toxin moves throughout the plant and poisons the bores when they eat the rose flesh while not harming the plant. I would think any means you can improvise would work as long as it doesn't harm your rose!

Black spot - I used to deal with this much more when I watered my roses with sprinklers rather than the ground irrigation I now have. Black spot occurs when water is left on the leaves and causes the leaves to discolor, especially susceptible to plants with close-growing stems and leaves. The leaves develop yellow patches, followed by black spots (small) within the discoloring. When the leaf is thoroughly discolored, it falls to the ground or gets caught up in the branches, perpetuating the problem.

You'll often see black spots on densely foliaged roses, and they can be common on smaller miniatures and floribundas in moist locations, as their leaves are close to one another. Rose dust or powder will help with this problem, but I believe your beneficial bugs will suffer from using this method, as it is a chemical fungicide. So, stick with one or the other method for each season.

A more organic method, and one your garden will benefit from, is to trim discolored leaves, clear out all branches and leaves that look like they may be contributing to the problem, and remove branches that are crossing over each other and causing congestion. The more air you can get to circulate within the plant and around the branches, the better suited it will be to fight the moisture build-up.

If you can water directly on the ground instead of a method that gets the leaves wet, do this too. If not, change your watering schedule to early morning times, so the moisture can evaporate during the day, and the chance of it staying on leaves when the temperatures drop is lessened.

Lastly

Though these practices may seem like more work than you would care to do, they really aren't any more demanding than any other plant in your bed. People may believe roses are intimidating, either due to the myths surrounding their beauty or the responses of people who don't like thorns. I'll give them that. But if you think for even a moment, you might like a rose, go for it. The pay-back is ten-fold.

And for those of you who have planned a raised garden bed full of roses? You make my heart sing. From one rose lover to another, *let's share pictures!*

Chapter Summary

- The rose has many myths that may keep gardeners from enjoying their beauty and benefit within the garden.
- There is a perfect rose for every type and situation within your garden.

In the next chapter, you will see how having a greenhouse will support your raised bed gardens.

7

SEEDLINGS, CUTTINGS, BARE ROOT AND FRUIT TREES

If you are able to have a greenhouse, cold frame, or some other type of outside structure that can harbor plants easily and keep them safe from the elements, I am a bit jealous. Although I have a wonderful west-facing window in my kitchen that is often delegated to sunning my latest potted stem, having a dedicated area for such whims will always be my "next project" to tackle.

Several things need to be in place to have a functional and easy area for nursing young seedlings and tender cuttings as they grow: water, sunlight, and regulated warmth. If you lack any one of these items, you will have a place that demands more from you than is required while also denying your plants a needed resource.

Greenhouses, cold frames, conservatories, and sunrooms provide the gardener with a huge benefit - *the ability to control an environment beneficial to plants.* It's almost like skipping the cold season altogether if you can use a greenhouse to support your plants on their path to a bountiful production.

Plants in Your Greenhouse

Let's talk about the details of nurturing cuttings, seedlings, and bare-root plants inside a greenhouse environment and how you go about preparing each for optimal success.

Cuttings

Depending on the type of plant, cuttings can be an ideal way of creating another separate plant from the host. By taking a sturdy, young stem, you are encouraging roots to sprout and create a new, regenerated plant. Roots can be stimulated by either a nick in the side of the stem or by removing a "node" from the stem. Dipping the exposed stem flesh in water, then in a root starter (usually a combination of vitamin B and other stimulating nutrients), and then gently setting the stem into a watered, prepared pot (I use fir mulch) will get most cuttings off to a great start. Top the pot with terrariums, such as a liter plastic bottle cut off at the bottom (cap side up) or another form of clear protector that will form a terrarium of sorts. You will want to make sure to trap moisture in and keep the prepared soil moist while supporting the growing root system.

Seedlings

After you've taken the time to buy, plant, water, and pamper your seeds along, the reward of having seedlings feels like becoming a new parent!!! But don't get too attached to the little guys. Usually, most seed instructions suggest planting several seeds in one hole for "thinning out" after they have sprouted.

Which is exactly what you have to do.

It always broke my heart to pull those little stems from the ground they worked so hard to break through, but thin you must. If you don't, *all* the small, tender starts will die due to lack of space, moisture, and light. Even though you may water a bit more or make sure they are getting enough light due to their fine structure, these little plants don't have much energy to "search" for the elements they need, and dodging other stems to grow far enough to outreach the other seedlings isn't in their capacity yet.

So thin the little ones to whatever your package instructions suggest, knowing the survival of the strongest plants will soon be able to offer blooms and grow sturdy throughout your season.

As your seedlings grow, you will be able to water them with a bit more ease than misting with the very gentle spray as they emerge. While they are fragile when young, they gain strength quickly. Keep them in good light, consistent temperatures, and feed according to suggestions.

Bare Root -

When I was very young, I remember going into my first root cellar with my mom when she was searching out, of course, bare-root roses. Before container growing became so prevalent, buying plants "bare root" was a sure way to find healthy, strong, and well-grown plants. You didn't just see the new buds promising the season's growth; you could also inspect the root system to make sure the roots were untrimmed and prolific, and ensure that there was no mold or fungus growing.

As the name implies, bare-root plants are not in the soil and are only the plant, from the tip of the stems to the ends of the roots. They are often in a semi-dormant state, ready to be planted in the soil when the soil is workable, and the weather promises warmer temperatures.

Nowadays, it's hard to even find a root cellar from which to buy plants. I know of several places in central California, but these only offer plants to those who come to their cellars. Moreover, you have to "beat out" the planters, whose business is to trim the roots, pot and label the plants, and sell for the largest portion of the nursery's market – *retail nursery perennials.* If they establish the bare-root plants for a year or more, you could consider yourself lucky.

Quite a few mail-order nurseries ship their stock as bare-root to reduce shipping costs.

The plants also seem to travel better after being stored dormant for a bit before shipments.

Instructions for these plants usually involve a brief hydration period and then immediate planting into the soil for the best results. Keeping these plants in a consistent and well-hydrated atmosphere will allow them to rejuvenate quickly and begin to sprout growth. Don't consider moving them outside until they have produced quite a bit of foliage and are stable in their container or temporary bed. Moving a bare-root plant into the elements too soon will cause stunted growth and low production of foliage, with no chance of blooms, either for visual appreciation or crop pollination.

When temperatures have evened outside, or you have taken measures to protect your bare-root plants from varying temperatures, you will be able to transplant them to your raised beds or containers.

Don't rush this step.

If they are ready, by all means, move them out, but if you have any reservations, hold on to the transplanting for a week or two. Your plants won't be any worse for wear, and you will be sure your plants are ready for production. If you are transplanting into a container, don't forget to put a well-draining medium in the bottom of the container, such as gravel, cocoa shells, or broken crockery.

Plant Forcing

Though everyone probably understands what forcing a plant indoors is, having a greenhouse or hothouse at your disposal gives you the benefit of having summer, no matter the season or weather outside. You can grow poinsettias for Christmas, tulips for Easter, fresh corn in May, or potatoes in June. With a greenhouse, you are Mother Nature herself and can dictate your harvest time according to your whims.

By having a greenhouse to start your raised bedding plants, you are providing them the best of all worlds before they are transplanted, as well as when they are transplanted into your raised bed. They will have a jump start in size, strength, health, and maturity. Not all plants have it so good. It's no wonder most entrants in the State or County Fair have discovered beginning their champion plants in a greenhouse leads to first place ribbons at the fair!

Management and Maintenance

Several things must be in place in order to manage a greenhouse successfully.

A consistent temperature and humidity level are necessary when forcing plants, whether you are starting bulbs in winter for spring bloom (because you forgot to plant them last fall?!) or want a long-season crop to mature in your beds (think long season vegetables such as beefsteak tomatoes, watermelons, and mammoth pumpkins). You are striving to provide optimal conditions for the plants' health. Doing anything less is a waste of time and effort because greenhouses are not for the meager bank account.

You also must have a convenient and sufficient water supply. Many commercial greenhouses have automatic systems with mist sprayers that offer the best conditions for seedlings and mature plants alike.

Just because the professionals have all the money-sucking devices doesn't mean you can't produce healthy plants on a budget. Your plants can be healthier and stronger, if only because you are focusing your care on fewer plants.

Make sure you have several options for watering your plants. There are hose nozzles with different settings for each stage of your seedlings and plants, from a light mist to a gentle spray. You'll also want a strong stream to clean off spilled dirt or plant debris.

It will also be to your benefit to decide on a plant feeding system, even if it is a water-soluble attachment to your hose. Your young plants will need food, and the easiest way for them to get those nutrients is the easiest way for you to assimilate them. If your feeding method is inconvenient or cumbersome, you will have a harder time using it, and most likely, won't feed your plants as often as you should.

Areas must also be accessible. If your greenhouse is large, keep rows of plants narrow, so you can reach across the trays and rows without hindrance. If you have a smaller greenhouse, make sure you can see the trays easily, and reach several levels if necessary.

If you have trellised plants, keep the structures sturdy, but also consider whether you will be transferring them when your plants are ready for the raised bed. You will probably also want them nimble and easy to move with your plants, knowing you can always substantiate them when you move them over to your raised box.

As light is rarely a problem in a greenhouse, you may have to pay attention to having too much of it. Sometimes the strength of sunlight will burn the leaves of tender plants, so be aware of any strong areas of direct sunlight before it becomes a problem, burning your seedlings or heating your greenhouse too much.

Add ventilation, if it isn't already part of your building, even if it means pulling out a windowpane or two to get a breeze going. If it gets too hot for your plants, they will suffer, and all your extra effort of preparing and working in your greenhouse will be wasted.

Container Plants and Trees

Many plants and trees are able to thrive within a greenhouse year-round. Bougainvilleas, lemon trees, avocados, and passion vines can all be grown in a greenhouse and introduced to the patio or porch when the season warms. I had three bougainvilleas I used to move from the patio to the living room window for over 20 years. They began to bloom at the beginning of the year and go crazy until the leaves fell and the days grew shorter. It was a wonderful way to bring my garden into the home. I did it, and you can too!

If you live in a temperate climate, you will be able to have these wonderful plants on your patio year-round. Imagine an avocado tree on the corner of your front porch or a Mandevilla climbing up the corner of your arbor. No longer do you have to worry about a

vivacious vine disturbing your home's foundation. Having it contained in a large pot or planter box means you can enjoy a beautiful wisteria along your home's back wall while curbing its vigor in a container.

If you are considering a permanent or moveable container plant for your porch or patio, make sure the plant or tree you are purchasing is from a reliable nursery. Trimmed root systems, lightweight soil, and sacrificed plant stock only expected to last a few weeks have no place in your garden plan of container gardening. Double-check the following details before purchasing.

- The roots of your plants have plenty of room to grow; plants aren't root-bound.
- The foliage must be pest-free and thriving, with new shoots and buds.
- The soil must be well-drained, giving your plant the optimal conditions to absorb water and yet drain out easily.
- The container must fit your purpose well, meaning you can easily move your plant from one area to another without harming the plant or your back! I have mine on a rolling dolly, with good sturdy wheels and a solid base to not tip if I hit the door jam or threshold unevenly.
- If your plant is being planted in a container permanently, make sure the container is big enough to enable the plant to grow for many seasons without being crowded or top-heavy or until you get it to its permanent spot.

You also need to take into consideration the growth of the plant. Don't think your lemon tree will always be 1½ foot high. If you take care of it, and you will, it will grow, just like the tomatoes and foxglove. You will most likely need to transplant it at some point, especially if it is in a pot that doesn't breathe well or is crowding the roots. Talk with the grower or nursery center personnel. They may be able to transplant it before you take it home to give you a few more years between transplants.

Consider espaliering your tree if it will be freestanding or by a bare wall or fence. Fruit trees, as well as vining plants, easily adapt to being trellised in a particular pattern and are beautiful ways to spruce up a bare fence or create interest on an ugly wall. If you have a fruit tree or crop-bearing vine, it will ease the harvesting, as you won't be picking from a ladder or bending to find hidden edibles.

Chapter Summary

- Plants are highly adaptable and can be trained into shapes, production quotas, and blooming season.

- By having a greenhouse or cold frame, growing seasons can be lengthened substantially.

In the next chapter, you will learn how to put your raised beds to rest for cooler season changes.

8

PREPPING, MAINTAINING, AND PLANNING FOR THE NEXT SEASON

W hat to keep, what to toss?

The blooms have come and gone, the harvest is in, bottled, canned, and preserved, and the leaves are falling from the trees. A few cold snaps have slipped in at night, signaling the finale of your raised bed garden.

What now?

It's time to put your plants to rest, clear out the debris and dead leaves, and turn the soil a few times.

If you are weathering over a container or two, you've probably already brought them inside and picked out the perfect spot for them to stay warm while the storms pass outside.

Winterizing a Raised Bed

If you just initiated your raised bed this season, your nutrients haven't been depleted too much. A good turning of the soil after you've removed all the dead plants and roots will give it more breathing space and deter mold or fungus from growing. This is particularly important if you've used quite a bit of organic matter in your soil, such as compost or manure. These conditioners, though very good for the plants and warm soil, can harbor spores that love to dig down and grow in "heated" organic soil when it's cold above ground. By lifting it and turning it over a few times, you will have aerated the matter and given it over to the cooler air, so the spores aren't protected.

You may want to add a low phosphate, even fertilizer, to the soil, keeping the nutrients in place for your plants next year. Sprinkle a handful or two on top of the soil before you till or shovel and turn the soil. This gets the fertilizer down where the roots will need it next year and saves you a bit of work next spring when the dirt might be a little on the frozen side under the top layer.

Composting

Composting has become a wonderful way to economically support your garden and use organic waste from the kitchen, which decays and builds a nice, rich additive for your beds.

When composting, be sure not to add "hot" compost to your bed, no matter what the season. Many think that by adding this soil to their garden before winter, it will have a final chance to decompose further and be ideal for the next spring. This idea is far from the truth.

When compost piles are hot and then "steam," they've built up gases that are growing and developing by-products, thereby releasing the gases into the air. This gas is a perfect place for spores and mold to begin their reign on your compost pile, and eventually, your garden bed if you put it on while it is still "growing."

Compost piles do get hot, and they do steam. The key is to let them continue to decompose, turn them often, and keep air circulating around the matter to maintain a "clean" compost and deter spore and fungus growth.

Keeping Your Beds Clean

I've also seen people cover their raised beds to keep seeds and leaves from getting into their pristine soil. If you cover your soil with anything, consider the possibility of trapping something in there that you won't want next season. These can be seeds from weeds that may have blown in at any time during the growing season or while you turned your back to take out the trash. In other words, you will never prevent weeds or their seeds from getting into your beds and boxes. By trapping them under a protective cover, you may just be giving them the extra strength they will need to attack with a vengeance next season. Be wary when attempting this process.

The secret to having and maintaining pristine raised beds is to place plants in a slightly tighter formation when planting next year. Doing this will discourage seeds from getting light and germinating while also keeping your soil soft and crumbly, so if you do have a weed or two, they will be easy to remove. Strategically plan your beds for next season, with taller plants in the back of the box where the seeds will most likely land and not germinate due to the taller plants allowing less light for the seeds to grow.

Aerate

If you have a pitchfork, this works wonders in several ways.

- It's easier to break up dirt clods, especially if your soil has a tendency to lean towards a clay base
- It's easier to add or remove mulch and debris
- It's easier to aerate your soil when turning it

Aerating with a pitchfork is a wonderful way to break up soil and get deep to let the soil breathe. Indeed, shovels turn soil well, but if your soil has any clay in it, this can form a smooth surface from the force of your shovel and often give more trouble and less aeration.

If your soil forms clumps and balls easily, get yourself a pitchfork. You and your plants will be happier!

Supplements - Fall Feeding vs Waiting

I mentioned earlier to till in some low-measured nutrients or fertilizer when you are turning the soil, and I truly believe in this.

But if you are only going to do one, either supplementing in the fall or the spring, *supplement the soil in the spring*. It is when you know the plants will need it, and it is much better to be sure of when the plant food is available to your plants than guessing if it is. Fall supplementing does improve soil, but it is a long-term benefit. So, if you are only feeding your plants, pick the spring.

Self-seeding Plants and Continual Growers

You may be in a temperate zone and won't have to remove plants, which get trapped under the snow and harbor organisms and spores. If this is your case, you are indeed blessed.

Because you have a longer growing season, you may not want to totally spade till your soil, especially if you have bi-annuals (plants that come up every other year) or self-sowing vegetables and perennials.

You will want to make sure the ground is loose throughout the season and clear of weeds before the season turns cooler. Your preferred plants have spent a huge amount of energy, and when the days begin to shorten, they move into a semi-dormant stage that still may see production, but certainly not at a pace seen in spring, summer, and fall.

If the plants get straggly, cut them back or pull them out. If they are perennials or annuals that can weather the cooler temperatures, feed sparingly to give them a bit of a rest from producing blooms and crops. In the spring, cut plants back and feed well to stimulate their growth cycle.

Chapter Summary

- Winterizing your raised bed will save you time next spring while avoiding problems that arise during "hibernation."
- Self-seeding plants need special care to keep them producing year after year.

In the next chapter, we will wrap up all the ideas you've learned, plus experiment with a few new ones.

FINAL WORDS

Outside the Box

Whether you have one raised bed or have decided to dominate your landscape with raised garden boxes, you are choosing a wise, low-maintenance, and easily controlled environment in which to grow plants and design a landscape. No matter if they are herbs, corn, rose gardens, or water-featured rock gardens, raised beds will give you a unique form of gardening as well as interesting diversity within the landscape.

As raised bed gardening is becoming more and more popular, the options for creating a raised bed are only limited by the imagination. The term "raised bed garden" has now reached cityscapes as well as multi-level and proportionate farming.

On these final pages, I'd like to discuss some varied designs of this diverse way of gardening to inspire your creativity. Moving toward new and exciting ways to make your garden and outside environment reflect your personality and vision can improve your harvest production and ornamental aesthetics. Now that you've mastered the basics, why not take it to the next level?!

As you can see, this landscape has used raised beds to provide wide walking paths and defined beautiful cutting gardens and plantings. Using raised beds in this manner allows the gardener to keep intruders out while still being able to enjoy the beauty of the beds. It depicts organization while still giving the plants an informal look.

In this raised box, the gardener combines vegetables, perennials, and annuals while providing interest and lush vegetation. The beds are simple but evoke continuous style and connectivity to the rest of the landscape. If the top border of the box were wider, it could also double as extra seating.

Here, the gardener has lineated paths leading to other areas of the design, giving glimpses of what's around the corner (or rhubarb!), creating curiosity and movement through the design.

In this raised bed, the gardener has created a balanced design, with walkways to amble on for contemplation, closer viewing, and design interest.

Using pathways between beds, this gardener creates a flow from space to space, which is appealing to the visitor while simplifying the maintenance and upkeep of the landscape. Beds are simplified, walkways are ample and pleasant, and each season creates a new view for enjoyment.

This design has raised beds within raised beds, working with levels to create interest and give height to the landscapes. Blooming gardens aren't the only plants you can use.

Having corn in the higher beds would give you privacy, while cabbages close to the edge and tomatoes in the middle provide variance and definition among the beautiful areas.

Looking out onto this yard in the morning brings the outdoors in and creates a calm and organized garden, using containers and raised beds from the front of the yard to the back fence. Plants can be moved as the weather or designer sees fit, giving more options for design and use.

Once again, a raised bed within a raised bed lessens work, offers a unique personality, and transforms a landscape as the seasons change. The height and density of plants can offer more options as the gardeners' skills also progress, thereby keeping ever-changing options alive.

Water features can be added in the center, a high-maintenance lawn can be reduced, or shapes can be moved for continual interest and enjoyment.

By inserting a raised bed into this large, open space, this gardener has created not only interest but opportunity to grow beauty. Be aware of areas that have proven to be problems and see if a raised bed could give you a growing area for blooms, vegetables, a specimen tree, or a hedge for privacy where none has been before.

This garden box welcomes homeowners and visitors alike with a beautiful perennial garden. The plants here will only fill in the area more each season and offer lush foliage and serenity to an otherwise dry and barren scene.

Without the raised beds in the middle of this view, the landscape would look like a fairway for a golf course, showing vistas but creating little interest. Here, the raised beds draw the eye (and curious onlookers) to meander from one beautiful area to the next. The height creates interest, the flowers provide color, and the spaciousness draws the viewer to uncover surprises beyond.

Soft colors draw the eye down this raised bed, providing a lovely scene. By planting the flowers closely, they also offer the gardener ease of maintenance by blocking out weed seeds and germination. The perennials and self-seeding plants offer additional ease in bed upkeep.

Using levels up or down from the viewing areas creates beauty and interest, whether the landscape is in hot weather climates or lush forest glens. Not only could you strengthen the height of a raised bed, as has been done in these terraced boxes with the cactus, but you could tumble vines over edges and border trees at an edge or two.

As we've talked about before, a raised bed doesn't have to be conventional or static. Rocks configured in multiple levels create a natural-looking bed while giving plants crevices to fill and gather water. Mosses and ground covers thrive in small areas, while a bird bath or miniature flowering tree provides nourishment for birds and wildlife.

Here we have a more conventional design, but the use of multiple level beds gives it interest and a unique design regardless of traditional squares or circles. By mixing up sizes, shapes, and heights, you create interest and make the landscape interesting, appealing, and fun.

Use elements within your raised bed to give it personality. This wagon wheel is whimsy and fun, but a gnome poking out from under a large bamboo patch or a resin garden rabbit hiding amongst the carrots could also bring smiles and frivolity.

Turn a problem area into beauty and function. Use landscape boxes and walls to bring you more space for plantings as well as providing beauty.

By lining stairs or stacking rocks, you can have a new and beautiful area instead of a slope of hard-to-mow lawn or ever-dry plants.

Lastly, using raised beds and pathways are wonderful ways to create "rooms" within a yard and landscape. Twist them, and incorporate curves into the beds. Doing this gives you a secret garden while also easing the necessities of yard work and maintenance. This gives you more time to enjoy your yard and lifestyle while your yard thrives and grows.

Having raised beds can give you a new outlook to all your yard, garden, vegetable, and design options. The controlled environment raised bed gardening eases your work level while lessening plant stress and demands. Giving them, as well as yourself, the convenience of raised bed gardening is a win-win on all fronts!

You've now come full-circle and can be classified as a *gardener*, entering one of the most caring and popular cultures in today's world. Not only are people anxious to grow and become part of a plant's life cycle, but enjoying the bounty of growing your own food or admiring your beautiful blooms brings a sense of awe and wonder to us all.

You now know how to -

- Build a sturdy raised garden box
- Prepare well-balanced and nutrient-rich soil for your plants
- Make educated choices for your own design and purposes
- Plant your bed for ultimate success
- Rejuvenate your boxes for continued success, season after season
- Maintain your garden with peak awareness of detrimental bugs and disease

- Extend your season for optimal performance and production

Enjoy your raised beds and experiment with plants and varieties as you learn and grow with your garden. You've taken the needed steps to master the art of growing plants. Now, experiment and unleash your creativity!

Customer reviews

5 star		0%
4 star		0%
3 star		0%
2 star		0%
1 star		0%

˅ How are ratings calculated?

Review this product

Share your thoughts with other customers

Write a customer review

I would be incredibly thankful if you could just take 60 seconds to write a brief review on Amazon, even if it's just a few sentences!

Just scan me!

A Special Gift To Our Readers

Included with your purchase of this book is Your Harvest Recipe.
You will be getting 15 very simple and easy delicious recipes as you work and do magic in your kitchen from your backyard's harvest!

Visit the link RIGHT NOW and claim your FREE bonus gift!

belletaylorbooks.com

For paperback versions only:
Scan the QR code for an access
to colored pictures!

REFERENCES

Image Credit: Shutterstock.com

Poindexter, J. (2019, November 30). *38 Perennial Vegetables & Fruits to Grow Once and Harvest Year after Year.* MorningChores. https://morningchores.com/perennial-vegetables/

Potts, L. P. (2019, August 9). *How to Get Rid of Fungus in Garden Soil.* HGTV. https://www.hgtv.com/outdoors/gardens/planting-and-maintenance/get-rid-fung us-garden-soil

The Editors. (2018a, June 11). *10 Beneficial Insects That Will Actually Help Your Plants.*

Good Housekeeping. https://www.goodhousekeeping.-com/home/gardening/a20705937/beneficial-insects/

The Editors. (2018b, July 10). *The 10 Most Destructive Garden Insects and How to Get Rid of Them.* Good Housekeeping. https://www.goodhousekeeping.com/home/gardening/a20705991/garden-insect-pests/

Made in the USA
Monee, IL
26 March 2022

ae295257-d990-4198-9758-883a9b92ab06R01